MW01493824

New Beginning Study Course
Connect The Dots And See!

MAINE-PATRIOT.com
3 Linnell Circle
Brunswick, Maine 04011

maine-patriot.com

New Beginning Study Course

"My people are destroyed for lack of knowledge." — Hosea 4:6.

New Beginning Study Course

"Study to show thyself approved unto God, a workman that needeth not to be ashamed, rightly dividing the word of truth." — 2 Timonty 2:15.

New Beginning Study Course

New Beginning Study Course
Connect The Dots And See!

Contents

New Beginning Study Course

Introduction

The purpose of this *New Beginning Study Course* is to provide you with information and knowledge that you can use. Most of this information is documented. Some of it is Theory; most of it is Fact.

We live in a world of fiction, in the Land of Oz, where Fact is hard to find. The information contained in this Study course will help you see the *difference* between Fiction and Fact.

This Study Course is designed to help you realize that we are beings who are free, who can create our world and be responsible for the events that occur in our lives. This is who we can be — *and who we really are.*

It is not the purpose of this Study Course to present unchangeable truth, for each individual is ever-changing his world, on a daily basis.

This information is for you — information you can prove for yourself — to enhance your understanding and awareness of events. This information will help to free your mind, so that you can create what you need and want.

This information will *empower* you; if you want to be empowered; or you can choose to remain in your present state, if you wish. This too is OK. It's a choice you have.

You are a being who is free!

New Beginning Study Course

1
Your New Beginning

This is a "New Beginning"; a fresh look at the world and yourself. Rather than raging at the world you see, it is *more* important to look at yourself, and see how you are meeting the challenges that the world presents.

This *New Beginning Study Course* is at once, commercial, political, secular, social and spiritual. This is a "practicum"; not just Theory and Talk. It's a laboratory of ideas and practices that you can test in the world around you, today.

Along the way, you will discover a wealth of ideas that has always been yours but that you didn't know existed. You didn't know, so you had no right to this wealth. Even if you *did* know it exists, but do not know how to work it, you have no legitimate right to this knowledge and wealth.

This *New Beginning Study Course* is a tool you can use to bridge the rivers of deception, illusion, ignorance and apathy that you might face. This *Course* will aid in opening your eyes, your mind, and your heart, to the marvelous gift of being you.

The purpose of these Lessons is to provide information to those who care enough about the things we face today, and will do something about it. This information will help you see the difference between Fiction and Fact; the facts of what actually is.

These Lessons are designed to help you realize that *you are a free being with unlimited potential who can create your own world, and be responsible for the things that occur in your life.* This is who you really are. But to the extent that you think you're *not responsible for the things that occur in your life,* to that degree you are enslaved by your own thoughts.

Connect The Dots And See!   11

Here is a quote that applies to you. Morpheus is talking to Neo, for the first time. *(From the movie, The Matrix).*

Morpheus: "I imagine right now you feel a bit like Alice, tumbling down a rabbit hole.

"You have the look of a man who accepts what he sees and is expecting to wake up. You're here because you know something that you can't explain, but you feel it.

"There is something wrong with the world. You don't know what it is, but it is there, *like a splinter in your mind.* It is this feeling that has brought you to me. Do you know what I'm talking about?"

Neo: "The Matrix."

Morpheus: "Do you want to know what it is?

"The Matrix is everywhere; it is all around us, even now in this very room. You can *see* it when you look out your window or turn on your television set. You can *feel* it when you go to work, when you go to church, when you pay your taxes. It is *the world of Oz* that has been pulled over your eyes to blind you from the truth, Neo; that you are a slave.

"Like everyone else, you were born into a prison that you cannot see, that you cannot smell, nor taste, nor touch. *A prison for your mind.*

"Unfortunately no one can tell you what the Matrix is. You have to see it for yourself. This is your last chance. After this there is no turning back.

"**Take the *blue* pill,** and the story ends; you will wake up in your bed and believe whatever you want to believe.

"**Take the *red* pill,** and you will stay in Wonderland (*in a wondrous land*) and I will show you how deep the rabbit hole goes. Remember. . . What I am offering you is *the truth,* nothing more.

"Follow me . . ."

We *do* live in such a world. And for anyone who has been involved in the system, to any degree in court, or with county, city, or national rules and regulations — or a bankruptcy or a foreclosure, you know something is very wrong.

You look all about you and see the morals of this country slipping into depravity. Many people are in despair. Nothing seems *real* anymore, and we can't put our finger on the cause. Something is wrong with our world. It bothers us, *"like a splinter in the mind."*

This book, *as with "The Matrix" itself,* will be a life altering experience for you. You will come to see that *we are commercial slaves.* This book will show you how we became slaves, and how we can free ourself from this slavery. This will affect everything you think and say and do. This will expose the Beast, and show you the Promised Land.

The world around you has been designed to distract you from the truth. Throughout your *entire* lifetime *others* have taught you the meanings of words, **with words.** But did you ever take the time to learn the *meanings* of these words for yourself?

This world is filled with symbols whose meanings you do not know nor understand. Words taught to you *verbally by someone else.* Your life is *filled* with meanings that quite simply are not true. It's a wonder that we can communicate with one another at all.

Are You In Commerce?

One of the main words we wish to define is *Commerce* and its various derivatives. Why? Because we live in a *sea of commerce* and are controlled by *maritime law.* We have lived so since our fleshly life here began.

Even lawyers, the courts, and law enforcement officers of this nation seem to be blind to the fact that we are controlled by and live in a *sea of Commerce.* Or they are trying to deceive us concerning the truth.

Each time anyone brings up *Commerce* in the courts, the attorneys and the judges exclaim *"We're not in commerce here. Commerce has nothing to do with this court. We're under statutory law."*

They appear to be so sincere, so positive.

It makes you wonder if they are *really* ignorant of this fact, or if they are *intentionally* deceiving us as good actors.

Whatever the reason, they *deny* that we are under the jurisdiction of Commerce, *when we are immersed in Commerce.* Therefore, we must have an understanding of what this means and how it affects us, regardless of the *ignorance* or the *deceit* of the courts of law.

Commerce: - *An interchange of goods or commodities; an engagement; sexual intercourse; intellectual or spiritual interchange; communion; merchandise; goods; trade.*

Commerce: - *To exchange goods, productions, or property of any kind; the buying, selling, and exchanging of articles. Intercourse by way of trade and traffic between different peoples or states and the citizens or inhabitants thereof, including not only the purchase, sale, and exchange of commodities, but also the instrumentalities and agencies by which it is promoted and the means and applications by which it is carried on, and the transportation of persons as well as goods, both by land and sea. The term "commerce" means trade, traffic, commerce, transportation, or communication among the several states.*

Commerce is dependent upon two related words: *value* and *scarcity.* Without these two aspects commerce falls flat and is unable to function. Create *scarcity* of anything and its *value* tends to soar. Decrease *scarcity* — by increasing supply — and you decrease *value.* This is how the power elite control our actions today, by controlling *scarcity* and *value* in commerce. **Scarcity,** by controlling supply. **Value,** by controlling demand.

When money is scarce, we fear that we do not have enough money. However, *it is the "lack of money" that we fear,* therefore worshipping (*giving worth to and value to*) the God of Fear.

The derivation of the word *worship* is "to create worth."

What part of your life is not affected by commerce?

The Entire Program

This program consists of eight study issues. Each issue illustrates a single state of your being; where and how, and who you are.

You and everyone else are in some state of being. There are specific procedures of advancing out of your present state into the next and higher state of being.

These procedures are part of every activity, and they must be complied with whether you know or understand them or not.

Following these procedures will take the chance out of everything you do, whether in business, personal finances, or in your individual life. The variables are only how well you perceive the situation and how much *energy* you apply to its practice.

The proper application of the procedures work no matter how they are applied, so long as the *right* procedure is applied in this sequence of steps taken.

Knowing the steps carries the responsibility of *using* them — or chance or fate prevails.

New Beginning Study Course

2
What You See Counts

Explorers were in route to the New World, sailing around the tip of Africa in massive ships driven by large canvas sails. They anchored their ships a safe distance offshore and used open long boats to row a small crew ashore. Never having seen white men nor their ships before, the natives asked the men how they arrived in that part of the world. The sailors pointed to the ships anchored offshore with the large white sails.

The natives looked in that direction, and no matter how hard the natives tried, they could not see the ships apart from the clouds.

The shaman of the tribe began to try something new. In looking at things differently, the image of the ships began to appear in his view. As he began to see things this way, others began to "see" the ships too. Within a brief period of time, everyone in the tribe could see the ships — *even those who were not there to meet the crew as they rowed ashore.*

The tribe had learned *a new way to "see" (perceive),* and in doing so, extended the boundaries of their world.

"Elisha prayed, and said, Lord, I pray thee, open his eyes, that he (his servant) may see. And the Lord opened the eyes of the young man; and he saw: and, behold, the mountain was full of horses and chariots of fire round about Elisha." — II Kings 6:17.

It becomes increasingly important now, more than ever, that your beliefs be not limited by what you have been taught. You are learning to trust yourself, your own feelings, and the process of your life.

In this world you have choices and free will.

You have the opportunity to realize your full potential as a divine expression of your creator, *to become a creator yourself,* by being aware of the power of righteous thought. Thoughts are "things"; not just pictures in your mind or sensations in your body.

As you think, you create. Is there ever a time you're not thinking? You are forever creating your experience with your thoughts!

"As a man thinketh in his heart so is he." — *Proverbs 23:7.*

You do not have to know the intricacies of the mind – only the ability to use them as they are designed. You can just "be," in the purity of your good intent.

This is the beauty of life.

You may choose to know more if you wish, or just "be" in your experience and the outcome will remain the same. The ability to create as a child of God is a skill available to everyone, — the result of *three components* of thought:

Clarity of thought

For thoughts to become manifest, they must be clear, concise, and sustained.

Constantly changing, wavering thoughts are incapable of sustaining a good result. They may appear as a series of incongruent, confusing situations, mirroring the blueprints of your mind.

"A double minded man is unstable in all his ways." — *James 1:8.*

Duration of thought

While clarity is the key component, unless it is sustained, the seed is not nurtured long enough to develop in the soil. *Persistence, alone, wins the prize.*

"...watching thereunto with all perseverance and supplication for all Saints." — *Ephesians 6:18.*

Intention of thought

Intention is the energy of thought that sustains the seed in the matrix of creation. The seed may dissolve at any point if the energy of intent is cast aside and lost.

"Be thou diligent to know the state of thy flocks, and look well to thy herds. For riches are not forever." — *Proverbs 27:23, 24.*

Meditation and Prayer

Meditation: - *meditate; akin to medicus, to heal, to cure; to care; to dwell on anything in thought; to turn over or resolve in creative Mind; to plan; to intend; to think on; close, or continued thought.*

Prayer: - *contemplation, an utterance, to ponder, to converse with oneself or with God ; to bind, to tie, to wind.*

Notice the similarities in the two words. Both concern thought. Both describe the action of *turning-over* or *winding-up* thoughts in your mind. To look at a thought from every angle by turning it over in your mind so that you can *see* it from different points of view, until you understand.

The difference between *prayer* and *meditation* is that *meditation* offers a silent space in which to hear the higher power ever talking to you. In *prayer* you are *speaking to God,* and in *meditation* you are *listening to "the still small voice" of the Holy Spirit.*

In either circumstance, you are seeking *intervention* from a "higher power" into a situation over which you feel powerless.

Traditionally, we have been taught to see ourselves as the created — not the creators of what we create. We feel separated from all else, and in that separation we cannot see, or identify with, the Power that creates. Feeling helpless to address the events that unfold in our lives, things seem to just happen by "chance."

A fundamental concept shared in the traditions of indigenous people is the idea that the human form is a part of creation, *not separate on its own.*

"Open the eyes of my heart, Lord, Open the eyes of my heart, I want to see you, I want to see you."

As an integral part of creation, the individual plays an important role in the cause of events within his world. These ancient concepts are just as valid today as they were thousands of years ago.

You are and always have been a part of all that you see.

You have the opportunity to plant and nurture your creation according to the thought patterns of the mind. You become the creator of your experience and impact the events of your world. You *intervene* on your own behalf, through your oneness with God, utilizing prayer and directed thought; or meditation.

To be or not to be; that is the question.

The way ancient native peoples such as the Australian aborigines, and American Indians, manifested their thoughts was by "being" that which they seek.

For example, if they wanted water or rain, they would *pray* rain; not pray *for* rain; but they would become the rain in thought. They would taste rain, feel rain, smell rain, hear rain, see rain, to the point that they would become the rain itself.

All senses activated in mind create a vacuum, if you will, so that the intended substance can manifest itself.

"Whosoever shall say unto this mountain, Be thou cast into the sea; and shall not doubt in his heart, but shall believe that those things which he saith shall come to pass; he shall have whatsoever he saith." — Mark 11:23.

A universal principal states that the physical universe cannot sustain a vacuum and will fill a seeming vacuum to balance itself. This is how you utilize the universal principles to your advantage.

The experience of each individual affects the whole, to a great degree. It is not enough to pray, for example, for *peace in the world.*

Praying for peace in the world may be well intentioned, but the request for peace in and of itself is incomplete. The highest form of *intervention,* that anyone may offer in a given situation, is not to *ask* for something to be, but rather *to see that which is desired.*

If *peace* is the desired reality, *peace* must become the reality in your experience. *You must see and become that peace.* It takes but few "reference points" within the whole to change the expression of the whole.

"As it is written, I have made thee a father of many nations (Abraham) *... who calleth those things that be not as though they were."* — Romans 4:17.

This is the lesson of native Africans and the Explorers mentioned at the beginning of this book.

Remember. . . Everything that you experience is part of your journey home: your "return." Don't be penalized for

"failing to make a return."

Each circumstance that you attract into your experience is the result of the energy you expend to bring *healing* to light; *of lack, limitation, want and woe.*

Try to become aware of anger, pain and frustration, from this point of view. Each is an expression of *fear.*

Take advantage of opportunities as they cross your path. You are more powerful than any *fear* that you might entertain. Fear is only a small fragment of your world.

Do not conform to duality, ego, or fear. You are an expression of God's love.

You are a child of God.

3
Chronological Events 450-1748

Commerce is a common thread woven throughout our entire history. *The merchant, the money changer, and the law of the merchant, are all parts of the laws of commerce,* or civil and maritime law.

This is not to say that *commerce* is bad. However, *commerce* brings with it the *laws of commerce; laws* that if not properly understood can bind you into slavery.

This happens only because we agree.

Banks create money out of thin air, called *credit,* and charge the people a profit called *interest* on the fiat money they create. Merchants who produce nothing at all sell what other people produce at a *larger profit* than the producer himself receives.

This happens only because we agree.

Merchants and bankers create laws through lawmakers they control, who protect commerce, and bind the people to obey the laws of commerce.

This happens only because we agree.

This happens because we trust other people to handle our own affairs. This has been happening throughout history.

There is great value looking at the past. The *patterns of the past* help us solve the *puzzles of today,* so we can better understand what's happening in our domain.

"A man with a knowledge of history may be said to have lived from the beginning of the world, continually adding to his knowledge in every way." *— David Hume: London "Of the Study of History" at page 390 (1898).*

A Chronology of the development of Law

450 - Peoples' Law: The Anglo-Saxons develope and extend the Law of the people.

1066 - Rulers' Law: The Peoples' freedom and natural rights are lost when England is conquered by the Normans from Normandy, France, and they become subject to the laws of ruling kings.

1215 - Magna Carta: The great struggle to restore freedom begins when King John is forced to sign the Magna Carta that guarantees unalienable rights to the people; The King must obey the Magna Carta as Law.

1265 - Parliamentary Power: The Principle "no taxation without representation" extends the powers of Parliament; all laws now require Parliament's consent, including the ability to impeach the Officers of the King.

1721 - Parliamentary Law: A Prime Minister is chosen to rule the Parliament, who chooses a cabinet and appoints the administrative officials with the King's consent. Thus, the British establish a Republic structured on Parliamentary Law.

1776 - Confederate Law: The Articles of Confederation are adopted to provide for individual "state law," with a Committee of the states functioning as a national Congress.

1787 - Constitutional Law: The American Founders establish a new kind of Republic — a system structured on Constitutional law.

The American colonies gained independence by force of arms and asserted their rights before the world by the Declaration of Independence prior to the Revolutionary War.

The Articles of Confederation (1777) were ratified four years later in 1781 and were soon replaced by a totally new system of people's Law under the Constitution for the United States (1787).

A Chronological timeline of world events

4000 B.C. - Genesis was translated from *Sumerian scripts* unearthed only decades ago in recently discovered Nineveh and other areas of the Tigris/Euphrates area of the Middle East. These ancient scripts, on baked clay tablets, date back to a civilization that was highly educated, incredibly organized, and socially advanced.

2123 B.C. - Abraham, grandfather of the Israelites, came from the ancient city of Nippur and later moved to Ur, both major cities of Sumer. Abraham was led by God to Haran, and finally to Canaan, where this "Promised Land" was to be inherited by his offspring, the Children of Israel.

2023 B.C. - Abraham's son Isaac is born (Genesis 21:5)

2000 B.C. - Babylon flourishes in the land of Sumer (Shinar). Babylon had canals to irrigate the land, indoor toilets, a city sewage system, public restrooms and baths, and a city to city postal system with baked clay letters and envelopes. Babylon had a judicial system where judges wore black robes just as they do today. Then they began to fall into disgrace but continued to rule *through fiction* until they were destroyed. They had a system of commerce that included coined money and Banks, Receipts, Titles, Seals, and Signatures. Merchant Law evolved into Roman Law then into Civil Law later becoming the Maritime Law of today.

1963 B.C. - Jacob is born to become Israel (Genesis 25:26).

1890 B.C. - Jacob's son Joseph is sold into Egyprtian slavery. (Genesis 37:2)

1833 B.C. - The Israelites flee to in Egypt because of Famine (Genesis 15:13, 47:8).

1513 B.C. - The Israelites are enslaved in Egypt, and Moses is born.

1433 B.C. - The Exodus — Moses leads the Israelites out of Egypt through the Red Sea into the wilderness.

1432 B.C. - God gives Moses the Ten Commandments for the Israelites (Exodus 20).

1393 B.C. - The Israelites reach the Promised Land and Moses dies.

1034 B.C. - Solomon begins building a temple at Jerusalem (1 Kings 6:1).

607 B.C. - Nebuchadnezzar, King of Babylon, captures the Israelites and takes them to Babylon in Sumer, now called Iraq.

539 B.C. - The Medo Persian, Cyrus the Great, conquers Babylon and allows some of the Israelites to go back to their homeland and rebuild the temple that Nebuchadnezzar had destroyed.

537 B.C. - The Assyrians hire *counselors* (attorneys) to frustrate the Israelites in building the temple, weakening their hands (Ezra 4:5).

"And hired counsellors against them, to frustrate their purpose..." — Ezra 4:5.)

525 B.C. - Alexander the Great captures Babylon from the Medes and releases the remnant of Israel back to their original homeland.

400 B.C. - The Hebrew language disappears, as a useful language, and the Israelites become scattered by repeated captures and enslavements by Assyria, hence "the lost tribes of Israel". Many believe remnants of the Israelite tribes wandered to northern Europe and carried the Biblical laws with them. Many think that America and Great Britain constitute the re-gathering of the lost tribes of Israel: Ephraim and Mannassa, Joseph's sons.

361 B.C. - Julian the Apostate (Flavius Julianus) begins his reign as Emperor of Rome and seizes Babylon from Assyria, adopting Babylonian Law (*Civil and Maritime law*) to Roman Law.

363 B.C. - Julian the Apostate reduces taxes by reducing court expenditures and eliminating corruption. He is killed in a battle with the Persians.

200 B.C. - Two Roman Emperors are assassinated for passing laws against usury.

133 B.C. - Babylonian priests turn over the priesthood to the Roman priests in Pergamos, in middle east Turkey, the future site of the "Seven Churches of Revelation" where *Pergamos is referred to as "Satan's Seat," or throne.* Babylon is destroyed but the Babylonian system remains, even to this day.

44 B.C. - Brutus, assassinates, Emperor Julius Caesar for minting coins to make money plentiful by opposing the money changers (the merchant's banks).

31 B.C. - Jesus Christ chases the money changers (the merchant's banks) out of the temple and three days later is charged with blasphemy by the Pharisees (the merchant's lawyers) and is crucified.

The Roman priesthood later moves from Pergamos to Rome.

From the beginning of America, the Bible was and is the foundation of American law. The Bible is the basis of all *real* law on the planet.

Prior to the eighth century, the Anglo-Saxon Europeans practiced most of the principles of the Bible that were the precepts of the people's law — a system designed to protect and preserve the unalienable rights of the people, and provide a balanced, limited form of government.

As one of the Founders of the Declaration of Independence, Thomas Jefferson, discovered, **Anglo-Saxon institutions** were almost identical to the ancient *institutions of Israel,* the oldest system of representative government known to man.

1000 - Goldsmiths as money changers (the merchant's banks) receive gold deposits and loan out more receipts than they have gold in reserve — hence fractional reserve banking is born.

1100 - Henry I takes the *money power* away from the money changers and establishes the *tally stick system* which lasts nearly 500 years.

1066 - The Normans, *under William the Conqueror,* subjugate the English people and establish the *royal dynasty* that occupies the throne of England today. The Normans impose a system of *rulership Law* that destroys their rights and confiscates much of their land, inflicting a system of cruel oppression that eventually becomes impossible to endure.

1215 - Because King John was one of the most cruel and ruthless of the Norman Kings, the Barons unite and force him to sign the *Magna Carta ("Large Charter")* at Runnymede, England (June 15, 1215), under the threat of being beheaded.

The Magna Carta returned to the people many of the rights that the conquerors had stolen from them, and acknowledged that the King himself is subject to the Magna Carta law.

The Magna Carta refers not only to the rights of the "Barons", but makes frequent reference to the rights of English "Freemen."

The American Founders consider themselves "Freemen" and invoke the Magna Carta — a covenant on the part of the King and his heirs — so that their rights will be respected as well.

The Magna Carta is one of the foundations of American law.

Parliament: - *a formal conference for the discussion of public affairs; a council of state in early medieval England; an assemblage of the nobility, clergy, and commons called together by the British sovereign as the su-*

preme legislative body in the United Kingdom; a similar assemblage in another kingdom or state; one of several principle courts of justice existing in France before the revolution of 1789.

Parliament means "a group of people who believe themselves to be superior by their own authority, making law in comfort and seclusion, without recourse or responsibility, to control the common people whom they consider to be of inferior quality and worthy of little regard."

So-called *aristocrats* do not want to communicate at the common level because it would endanger their self-appointed superior status as the Elite.

The foundations of parliamentary government began to develop around 1265, and this gradually developed into a legislative voice to represent the desires of the people. It also provided a bargaining tool to regain some of the lost powers of the people and to limit the tyrannical powers of the King, and to persuade the people not to resist the powers of the King.

The Parliament retained the right to have no taxation without the approval of the people's representatives. They also established the principle that there would be no laws imposed on the people that had not been first fully approved by the Parliament.

Finally, the Parliament secured the right to impeach abusive officers of the King whenever it was shown that they had violated the law in the exercise of their high office. A legislative forum is developed thereby.

1500 - Henry VII strengthens laws against usury which infuriates the money changers (the merchant's banks). Julius Caesar conquers England, paving the way, in England, for the Roman Catholic Church, which excommunicates the King for beheading his wives. The *succeeding* King drives the Roman Catholic Church out of England and institutes the Church of England.

1600 - Queen Elizabeth I controls the money supply and issues her own coin against the wishes of the money changers (the merchant's bank).

1649 - Oliver Cromwell is financed by the money changers (the merchant's bank) and has King Charles killed, and plunges England into debt, from wars, and takes over the City of London for his own use (Oliver Cromwell's District called London, just like Congress' District called Washington, D.C.).

1688 - The money changers (the merchant's bank) finance William of Orange of the Netherlands to overthrow the Stuart Kings and take possession of the English Throne, for them.

1694 - England is financially strapped after 50 years of war with Holland and France. The private Bank of England is formed to established laws to protect the bank, and confirm the debt of England owed to the Crown. The Bank of England replaces the *tally stick system* with its own *money system* and takes away the King's power to control money.

1698 - English debt grows from 1,250,000 million lbs. to 16,000,000 million lbs. within four years, an increase of 1,280%.

1748 - Amschel Bauer in Germany opens a goldsmith shop under the sign of Red Shield. (Rote Schild in the German tongue) (Rothschild)

Amschel Rothschild had five sons.

— — —

During the reign of two German Kings over England (*George I and George II from 1714 to 1760*), the Parliament was left relatively on its own more. The government was run almost entirely by the King's Prime Minister, which meant that he and the other members of Parliament, serving in his cabinet could have a relatively free hand in running the government.

This gave England a limited monarchy with a parliament system of government that allowed the legislature to exercise unlimited power

This parliament system never rose above this form, nor did its Commonwealths, Canada, Australia and the others that followed this same pattern. As a result, many Europeans began migrating to "America" to be socially and spiritually free.

America: - *the soil comprising the contiguous 50 states now called the united States of America. As of 1776 America comprised 13 independent colonies.*

America was at first an English colony where the people elected the delegates of local and provincial assemblies. This first occurred in Virginia, in 1619.

New Beginning Study Course

4
Chronological Events 1773-1980

As the colonies gained political and economic strength they eventually demanded their full rights as Englishmen, by issuing the **Declaration of Independence** from the King of England, which became a *declaration of war.* The colonists then confederated together as the United States of America — a confederated Republic wherein the States were supreme.

1773 - May, the British renew the *Townsend Act* that is about to expire and allows the *British East India Tea Company* to sell direct to the American public without American middlemen and any middle man markup, thus angering the merchant's of Boston and triggering the *Boston Tea Party.* On December 16, thirty men disguised as Mohawk Indians dump 342 chests of British tea into Boston harbor.

1774 - King George III and the British Parliament retaliate by passing the *Coercive Acts,* called by the colonists in America, the *Intolerable Acts.*

1774 - Summer, *actual Start of the Revolutionary War.* Massachusetts Colonists prevent the British courts from functioning in their State, and develope self rule.

1774 - The *first Continental Congress* assembles in Philadelphia.

1775 - April 18, the British are repelled at Concord, Massachusetts and are exiled to the Boston peninsular.

1776 - May 1, *The Order of the Illuminati,* a secret society of *wealthy intellectuals,* is founded by Dr. Adam Weishaupt, a Professor of Canon Law at Ingolstadt University, in Bavaria. After the headquarters of the Illuminati are raided by the Bavarian government, the Illuminati operate under the guise of the *League of the Just.* From the

Connect The Dots And See!   33

beginning, the Illuminati's purpose is to overthrow the Pope, all civil governments and the Kings of Europe.

1781 - The first national bank of the United States — the *Bank of North America* — is formed by an act of the *Continental Congress* that owns and controls it as a public institution in the public's name.

1787 - the *Constitution for the United States* is devised.

1789 - the *Constitution for the United States* is ratified by the colonial States.

1791 - The *Assumption Act* allows the newly chartered *Bank of the United States* (more commonly known today as the *First Bank of America*) to assume private control of state chartered banks.

1792 - The *Coinage Act,* which has never been revoked, defines a "dollar" as *a unit of weight* of either silver or gold. Federal Reserve Notes are NOT "dollars" even though this is stated on their face.

A Minnesota court case, in 1969, said:

"These Federal Reserve Notes are not lawful money within the contemplation of the Constitution of the United States, and are null and void. Further, the Notes on their face are not redeemable in Gold or Silver Coin nor is there a fund set aside anywhere for the redemption of said notes."

1832 - President Andrew Jackson vetoes renewal of the charter for the *Second Bank of the United States.* Two subsequent assassination attempts on his life prove unsuccessful when the pistol aimed at him misfires both times.

1871 - The Federal Government reforms itself into a *District of Columbia Corporation* called *Washington, D.C.,* and adopts itself under its new *"Constitution OF (not FOR) the United States of America."*

1873 - *Financial panic.*

1884 - *Financial panic.*

1893 - *Financial panic.*

1907 - *Financial panic* — This panic, *provoked by J.P. Morgan,* brings about a total change of the monetary system, and private control of the central banks.

1910 - The basic plan of the *Federal Reserve Act* is drafted in a secret meeting at the private resort of J.P. Morgan on Jekyll Island off the coast of Georgia. The seven men who attend represent an estimated *one-fourth of the total wealth of the world.*

They are:

1. **Nelson W. Aldrich,** Republican Whip in the Senate, Chairman of the *National Monetary Commission,* Father-in-law to John D. Rockefeller Jr.;

2. **Henry P. Davidson,** Sr. Partner of *J.P. Morgan Company;*

3. **Charles D. Norton,** President of the *First National Bank of New York;*

4. **Piatt Andrew,** Assistant Secretary of the *United States Treasury;*

5. **Frank A. Vanderlip,** President of the *National City Bank of New York,* representing William Rockefeller;

6. **Benjamin Strong,** head of J.P. Morgan's *Bankers Trust Company,* later to become head of the *Federal Reserve System.*

7. **Paul M. Warburg,** a partner in *Kuhn, Loeb & Company,* representing the Rothschilds and Warburgs in Europe.

1912 - April 15, 2:30 A.M., the 46,328 ton *R.M.S Titanic* with 2223 souls aboard, sinks after contact with an iceberg in the North Atlantic; only 700 or so manage to survive, more that 1500 people die. Many of the ultra wealthy on board are opposed to the above plans to establish a Central Bank.

1913 - April 8, the *17th Amendment* is ratified, passing power reserved to the States into the hands of *a new form of federalism,* placing the States of the Union in the position of *mere supervised fanchises* of such government. This Act sets the stage for the complete change of the Federal government from *a constitutionally guaranteed Republic to a Democracy,* and sets the stage for a hostile corporate takeover of the monetary system of the United States, placing it in private hands.

1913 - December 22, 23, *The Federal Reserve Act* creates the *Federal Reserve System of District Banks* — a non-federal private for-profit Corporation, signed into law by Woodrow Wilson, regarding which years later he confesses, *"I have unwittingly ruined my country."*

1915 - May 7, the *U.S.S. Lusitania,* an ocean liner with American passengers on board, is sunk by a German U-boat commanded by Captain Walther Scheieger, in the English Channel, off the coast of Ireland. Right before this happened, the *Lusitania,* reportedly carrying over six million rounds of ammunition owned by the *J.P. Morgan Company,* stopped its traditional zigzag sailing pattern and cut its speed in half to await an escort vessel, the *H.M.S. Juno,* which was to lead it to port. Unbeknownst to the *Lusitania,* and for reasons which have never been satisfactorily explained, the First Lord of the Admiralty, Winston Churchill, ordered the *Juno* to return to the port of Queenstown while the *Lusitania* sits alone and unprotected in the English channel waiting for its arrival. One torpedo is fired, and within 18 minutes 1,198 passengers including 128 Americans, perish. It is speculated that Churchill deliberately placed the *Lusitania* in danger in order to draw America into the war.

1917 - April 16, the United States officially declares war on the Axis powers.

1919 - June 28, *The League of Nations* is signed into existence without the participation of the United States, until more than twenty years later it is repackaged as *The United Nations.*

1920 - Financial panic - Financial panic is engineered by the FED, proving that it can manipulate the economies of nations at will, without war.

1921 - The *Sheppard-Towner Maternity Act* (known as the *Maternity Act*) creates the *Registration of Birth Records* — or what we now know as the *Birth Certificate.* This legislation authorizes federal aid to states for maternity, child health and welfare programs. However, the Supreme Court rules the act unconstitutional the following year, but the issuance of *Birth Certificates* remains.

1921 - July 29, *The Counsel on Foreign Relations* (CFR) is formed because the United States refuses to join the *League of Nations* following World War I. An outgrowth of a secret British society formed by Cecil Rhodes and backed by Rockefeller and Carnegie Foundation money, the CFR's agenda envisions nothing less than *world domination* and the establishment of a modern *feudalist society* controlled by themselves through the world's central banks.

1930 - the *Breton Woods Agreement in* which sixteen nations declare bankruptcy. The *Geneva Convention Treaty* declares that *International Bankruptcy Treaties* are superior to all federal laws and the *United States Constitution.*

1933 - March 9, President Roosevelt (*Rosenfelt*) declares **the *Bankruptcy of the United States*** by Executive Orders #6073, 6102, 6111 & 6260 as codified at 12 USCA 95a. See Senate Report 93-549, pages 187 & 594.

1938 - the Federal United States joins the <u>*International Criminal Police* Commission</u> (INTERPOL), designating the U.S. Attorney General as the official representative to the organization. The Secretary of the Treasury designated by the U.S. Attorney General becomes the representative to

INTERPOL in 1958. Pursuant to Article 30 of the *Constitution and General Regulations of Interpol* (22 USC § 263(a)), all representatives must *"renounce their allegiance to their respective countries and expatriate."*

1944 - July, the *Breton Woods Monetary Conference* at the Washington Hotel, in Breton Woods, New Hampshire, which through the guidance of Harry Dexter White, Assistant Secretary of the U.S. Treasury, later known as a member of a Communist espionage ring, and John Maynard Keynes, a well known *Fabian Socialist* from England, creates the IMF/World Bank whose main role is the elimination of the gold-exchange standard as the basis of currency valuation, and the establishment of *World Socialism.* White becomes the first executive director for the United States at the IMF/World Bank. Over 100 additional nations declare bankruptcy at this time. The World Bank is the agent for the **creditors/principles** of the bankrupt federal United States and is not subject to American Law.

1946 - the *Administrative Procedures Act* is instituted.

1973 - the *Trilateral Commission* is created by David Rockefeller to coordinate North America (*the United States, Mexico, & Canada*), Japan and Western Europe into a *New World Order* under slogans such as "free trade" and "environmental protection" until a full-blown regional government emerges from this process. The so-called "trade treaties" within the European Union (EU) — i.e., the *North American Free Trade Agreement on Tariffs and Trade* (GATT) — have little to do with free trade.

1980 - the *UNIDO Treaty* (Treaty No. 9719) is ratified by the Senate which makes the *United States Constitution* subservient to the *United Nations World Constitution.* UNIDO is the *United Nations Industrial Development Organization.*

5
That Country Must Be Destroyed!

Prior to the American Revolution commerce was done by barter or by *paper money* printed by the different States according to the production of goods and services by the people. The *Times of London* stated the following regarding the paper money and prosperity of America:

"If this mischievous financial policy, which has its origins in North America, shall become endurrated down to a fixture, *that government will furnish its own money without cost.* It will pay off debts and be without debt. It will have all the money necessary to carry on its commerce. It will become prosperous without precedent in the history of the world. The brains and the wealth of all the countries will go to North America. *That country must be destroyed or it will destroy every Monarchy on the globe.*"

Most people do not realize that the primary reason for the Revolutionary war was *not* "taxation without representation" but the forced payment of taxes to the King in gold, instead of in America's paper money.

America was flourishing by using its own "fiat money system" *based on production* — instead of a "gold based money system" that could be manipulated and taxed by the King.

The King could not "control" the "fiat money system" so he passed a law requiring everyone to pay taxes to the Crown only in gold. The King had most of the gold — the colonies had little (*scarcity = value*). Unemployment ensued and embittered souls cried out for *secession*.

In one sense, America won the Revolutionary war with England, but the money powers were waiting at the gate from the very start.

On the surface, the British Empire, as a world government, lost the American Revolution, but the power structure behind the Empire did not.

The most visible aspect of the power structure in America was the *East India Company,* owned by the bankers of the Crown, in London, England. This was a private enterprise whose flag had thirteen red and white horizontal stripes with a blue rectangle in its upper left-hand corner.

Betsy Ross had a pattern for her so-called "creative invention" of the stars and stripes — the flag of the international financiers. The true American flag has *vertical stripes* and a different design.

While the British government lost the war of 1776, the owners of the *East India Company* (the banks) — who made up most of the invisible sovereign power structure behind the British government — not only did not lose the war, but moved right in to the New American economy, — hand in hand with America's most powerful landowners of the day.

Constitutional Supremacy — The authority for the American Constitution:

Six documents became the basis and guidelines of our American Constitution.

A constitution must be based on some prior reference in order to be established. Any subsequent constitution based on this premise must have an enabling clause. No American Constitution established from this point on can diminish the rights already established in the *six documents* listed below:

1. **The Bible**.
2. **The Magna Carta** signed by King John in 1215.

3. **The Petition of Rights** granted by King Charles I in 1628.
4. **The Habeas Corpus Rights** granted by King Charles in 1679.
5. **The English Bill of Rights** granted by William and Mary in 1689.
6. **The Articles of Confederation.**

Next, the people of the various states created the state governments for the protection of their rights. They delegated certain powers via state constitutions to the three branches of government that were to carry out the constitutional dictate to protect those rights.

Then the States created the United States.

The American Constitution created a new structure of government that was established on a much different plane than the parliamentary system or that of the confederation of states.

It was a "constitutional republic" belonging to the States wherein a limited amount of power was belonging to the federal government, with the remaining power delegated to the states, or remaining with the people themselves.

The Constitution was designed and supported by the bankers and pushed through to enforce their control over the United States of America. Had the Articles of Confederation been improved, instead of the Constitution being devised, the bankers would have had far less control than they achieved.

Ten Square Miles

Columbia: - *Christopher Columbus; the UNITED STATES; originated in 1775; not the united States of America.*

The Columba faction: - *an Italian organization and Masonic group funded Cristoforo Colon and renamed him as Christopher Columbus (circa 1492).* The *Columba faction's symbol was a black dove. The Illuminati (also an Italian organization and Masonic group) was formed in 1776.* Both groups strictly adhere to their own hereditary bloodlines, and purposely do not intermix with other ancestries.

The *UNITED STATES INC* consists only of the ten miles square of Washington, D.C. and its territories of Guam, Samoa, Mariana Islands, and Puerto Rico, etc.

Plenary power: - *one of the powers granted to the congress in the federal constitution is in Article 1, section 8, clause 16 and 17:*

16. To exercise exclusive legislation in all cases whatsoever, over such district *(not exceeding ten mile square) as may, by cession of particular states, and the acceptance of congress, become* the seat of government of the United States, *and to exercise like authority over* all places purchased, *by the consent of the legislature of the state in which the same shall be, for the erection of forts, magazines, arsenals, dock-yards, and the needful buildings: ── and,*

17. To make all laws which shall be necessary and proper for carrying into execution the foregoing powers, and all the new powers vested by this constitution in the government of the United States, or in any department or officer thereof.

Congress has absolute or what is described as "plenary power": police power and the like.

Where does Congress have such plenary power? *Only within the geographical area of the District of Columbia,* and all forts, magazines, arsenals, dockyards, and other needful buildings within the several States.

The corporate UNITED STATES is an abstraction

The UNITED STATES exists only on paper. It is a total fiction. It exists only as an idea, whereas the various State Republics of the Union exist in substance and reality.

The United States takes on physical reality only after Congress activates 18 constitutionally delegated powers in accordance with Article 1 section 7 of the Constitution.

The U.S. Constitution is bifurcated

The Constitution is separated into two parts. It is separated from the original jurisdiction outlined in the Articles of Confederation.

Article 1, section 8, clauses 16 & 17 set this out.

The U.S. Congress has the right to make laws only regarding Washington D.C. — within its ten square miles — and the other territories owned by the UNITED STATES.

This limited scope of legislative powers is its *only* lawful authority relative to the people of the various states.

The First National Bank in the United States

One of the first acts that President Washington did was to declare a national emergency.

In 1781, Congress chartered the First National Bank for a term of 20 years, to the same European bankers who were holding the Confederate's debts *before* the war. The bankers loaned worthless, un-backed, non-secured, printed money to each other, to charter this first bank.

While thousands of lives were being lost fighting a revolutionary war to get control of our own money, why did our founding fathers (Congress) contract with the same bankers that instigated the Revolutionary War in the first place?

Simple. *They had to.*

Under public international law, Congress' Creditor (the Crown) forced the United States to establish a private bank to hold the securities as collateral for their loans.

Since the Crown (House of Rothschild) was the creditor of the constitutionally guaranteed loans, they demanded the establishment of a *private bank* to hold the securities of the United States as the assets pledged to the Crown in England to secure the debt on which the United States had defaulted.

The default of the United States was planned. Throughout history Babylon follows wherever we go.

European Bankers Expand

1785 - The youngest Rothschild, Nathan, expanded his wealth to 20,000 pounds in a 15 year period by using other peoples money. An increase of 2500%.

1787 - Amschel Rothschild made the famous statement:

"Let me issue and control a Nation's money and I care not who writes the laws."

Thomas Jefferson stated,

"If the American people ever allow the previous banks to control the issue of their currency, first by inflation then by deflation, the banks and the corporations which grow up around them will deprive the people of all property until their children wake homeless on the Continent their fathers conquered."

1798 - The five Rothschild brothers expand by opening banks in each of the major cities of Europe. Amschel Mayer: *Germany;* Solomon: *Vienna;* Jacob: *Paris;* Nathan: *London;* Carl: *Naples.*

The War of 1812 and the Second National Bank

Marque: - *A reprisal entitling one who has been wronged who is unable to receive ordinary justice to take the goods of the wrongdoer in satisfaction for the wrong. — Blacks Law 7th, 986.*

The charter for the first private United States bank was for 20 years, until 1811. What happened in 1812? The War of 1812. What did England attack? England attacked Washington, D.C., the ten square mile District where they burned the White House and other buildings and the government records of the 13th Amendment.

Was England's attack on the District United States an act of war?

No! The act of war, under public international law, was the District United States' refusal to renew the Charter of the First National Bank that held the securities on the unpaid debt that the United States Congress owed to the Crown.

When the *District United States* committed this act of war (not paying its lawful creditor what it owed in a peaceful manner), the only remedy open to the *creditor nation,* under international law, was to come against the *debtor nation* (the United States) on "letters of marque" and seize the *debtor nation's assets* to protect its loan.

Did the second national bank get approved? *Absolutely.* Right after the war, In 1816.

When England attacked the United States because of its loan default, the Americans suffered the penalty of not renewing the Charter of the national bank. The Charter for the Second National Bank of the United States was for another 20 years, until 1836.

The Forgotten 13th Amendment

Attorney: - *The attorney is obligated to the courts and the public. Wherever his duties to his client conflict with those he owes as an officer of the court in the administration of justice, the former duties must yield to the latter.* — *Corpus Juris Secundum, 1980, section 4 See note.*

All attorneys owe their allegiance, first to the *Crown in England* (*the House of Rothschild*), then to the courts, then to the public, and *lastly* to their clients. Is it any wonder your attorney never wins a case for you in court?

BAR: - *Acronym for the* British Accreditation Regency.

Attorneys are members of the BAR. The American Bar Association is a branch of the Bar Council, *the sole bar association in England.* All laws in America, today, are the copyrighted property of a British company, the Crown. All state Codes are private commercial British-owned "law."

All attorneys follow instruction from England. Attorneys twist and *turn-over (overturn)* their clients in synch with the private law of the bankruptcy. That is their job. That is their pledge to those to whom they have pledged allegiance.

By definition, the obligations and duties of attorneys extend to the court and the "public" (the government) before any mere "client." Clients are "wards of the court" and therefore "persons of unsound mind."

The Original 13th Amendment - One other important issue of the War of 1812

The original 13th Amendment prohibited esquire attorneys and anyone else with a title of nobility to hold any public office in America. All the states had ratified this 13th Amendment by 1812 except for Virginia.

The War of 1812 was waged mostly in Washington, D.C. The British burned all the repository buildings, attempting to destroy all the records of the new UNITED

STATES, situated in Washington, D.C.

The war of 1812 was partly waged to prevent the passage and enforcement of the original Thirteenth Amendment. Many other book repositories throughout the states were burned to the ground and all records destroyed as well.

As a result of the accumulated debt of waging that war and the bank-manufactured depression in the midst of the war, a new Bank Charter was issued in 1816 for another 20 years until 1836.

Andrew Jackson and the Bank

President Andrew Jackson refused to renew the second bank's charter in 1836. Jackson's reasoning was simple: *"The Constitution does not delegate authority for Congress to establish a national bank."*

Jackson's rationale has never been seriously challenged and the Constitution has never been amended to authorize Congress to establish a national bank. Nor, for that matter, does the Constitution delegate authority for the United States to establish corporations.

No national bank was established in America thereafter until 1913 and the Federal Reserve Bank. Andrew Jackson did an excellent job on his watch.

What did Congress do to Andrew Jackson? They fought him tooth and nail, because Congress is made up mostly of attorneys who owe their title of nobility to the Crown in England. Congress is populated with attorneys who are Esquire noblemen who owe their allegiance to the English Crown. So, who does our Congress represent? The international Bankers.

The bankers hired an assassin to kill Andrew Jackson, using two pistols, but the plot failed when both pistols misfired.

Andrew Jackson violated public international law in denying the creditor his just lien rights against the debtor.

However, the bankers did not lend value (substance) so they actually had *an unperfected lien,* therefore the law did not actually apply in this case.

Andrew Jackson stated,

> *"Controlling our currency, receiving our public money, and holding thousands of our citizens in dependence, would be more formidable and dangerous than the military power of an enemy."*

6
The Civil War & Its Aftermath

sine die: - *without day; with no day being assigned [as for the resumption of a meeting or hearing].*

On March 27, 1861, the Southern states declared their *states rights* pursuant to the Constitution and walked out of Congress. This created *sine die,* which literally means *"without day,"* with no day being assigned to reconvene. Congress adjourned without providing a date to reconvene. Abraham Lincoln had just been elected President, and Congress could not transact business without a quorum, so the *Constitutional Republic* was gone. Therefore, Lincoln declared martial law and ruled by *Executive Order under the war powers clause,* instead. Martial law has arguably never been ended and a *Constitutional Facade* has been maintained, ever since then.

Slavery was only window dressing for the Civil War. The War had nothing to do with slavery. It had to do with *States Rights* and the national debt to the bankers. The Southern States claimed their *release from their debt to the Crown,* as was their right. The North wanted to continue its debt and its credit opportunities with the Crown.

When the South walked out of Congress, this ended the *public side* of the bifurcated Constitution as far as the republic was concerned. What remained was the *private side* of the government; the *military democracy* under the dictated rule of the bankers.

The *de facto* 13th Amendment was enacted at the end of the Civil War, December 18, 1865. The 14th Amendment was enacted three years later, on July 28, 1868, and two years after that, on March 30, 1870, the 15th Amendment.

Commander in Chief, Abraham Lincoln proclaimed his first open threat to the bankers when he said:

"The government should create, issue, and circulate all currency and credit needed to satisfy the spending power of the government and the buying power of consumers. The privilege of creating and issuing money is not only the *supreme prerogative* of government, but it is the governments' *greatest opportunity.*"

Lincoln was assassinated a few weeks later because he defied the bankers by printing interest free money to pay for the war.

The New 13th Amendment freed the slaves from their previous owners and the 14th Amendment subjected the freed slaves to the ten miles square jurisdiction of Washington, D.C. instead.

The only people in the United States who had been under the jurisdiction of the private, bifurcated government of the ten square miles of Washington. D.C. were the government employees within the territories owned by the UNITED STATES INC. Now *the captive citizens of the South* and the former slaves became 14th Amendment citizens of the UNITED STATES.

The rest of the people could still invoke their people power over government through original jurisdiction of the Republic side of the Constitution. The government operates now *under the authority of private law* under the dictatorship of the *creditor banks.*

England incorporates the UNITED STATES

1871 - The default loomed again at the end of the Civil War [*the war against the southern states*] and bankruptcy was eminent, so England incorporated the ten mile square district UNITED STATES. They used the U.S. Constitution as the By-Laws of the district UNITED STATES; not as authority *under* the U.S. Constitution, but as authority *over* the U.S. Constitution. They copyrighted not only their new Constitution but also many names of the new corporation, such as the UNITED STATES, the UNITED STATES OF AMERICA, U.S., U.S.A., and other titles, as their own. This was the final blow to the original United States Constitution. Henceforth, the UNITED STATES INC. was governed entirely by *private corporate law* dictated by the *creditor banks.*

More Bankruptcy Re-organizations
1909 - The default loan looms once more. The US government asks the Crown in England for an extension of time. This extension of time was granted for another 20 years on several conditions. One of the conditions was that the United States allow the creditors to establish *a third private National Bank.*

1910 - The basic plan for *the Federal Reserve System* was devised in a secret meeting on Jekyll Island, off the coast of Georgia, at the private resort of J.P. Morgan, during the Thanksgiving Day Holiday in November. It met for 10 days from November 23, to December 3, 1910.

1913 - The *Federal Reserve Bank Act,* the *16th Amendment* (*income tax collection for the none-federal, Federal Reserve*), and the *17th Amendment* (*public election of Senators*), were the conditions for the 20 year extension of time on the loan default. The two Amendments ended the States' *power and rights* as the UNITED STATES adopted the Babylonian system of control.

1915 - The ocean liner, *U.S.S. Lusitania,* with American passengers on board, is sunk off the coast of Ireland. Now seen to be a false flag event staged to bring the United States into the *First World War.* (*See 1915, page 36*).

First World War

1917 - The UNITED STATES is drafted into the First World War. The debt of the UNITED STATES to the Crown accumulates so fast that it again becomes impossible for the federal United States to repay the debt in 1929. The war extends the war powers that Commander in Chief Abraham Lincoln put in place during his so-called "Presidency." Lincoln's war powers clause is expanded into *The Trading with the Enemy Act of 1917* wherein citizens of the United States of America are declared to be *enemies of the corporate UNITED STATES.*

The Great Depression

1929 - The stock market crashes and The Great Depression begins after the financial bubble of the Roaring Twenties bursts.

The stock market crash removed billions of dollars from the people to the banks. This also removed cash from circulation for the people's use. Those who still held cash invested in high-interest-yielding Treasury Bonds driven even higher by increased demand. As a result, even more cash was removed from circulation of the general public, to the point where there was not enough cash left in circulation to purchase the goods and services being produced.

Production came to a halt as unsold inventory overcrowded the marketplace. There were more products on the market than there was available cash to buy them. Prices plummeted and industries plunged into bankruptcy, throwing millions of people out of work and out of cash. Foreclosures on homes, factories, businesses and farms rose to the highest level in the history of the world. A mere dime, was literally a blessing to many families now living on the street. Millions of people lost everything they had to the bankers, keeping only the clothing on their backs.

1930 - the International Bankers in Europe declare many nations bankrupt, including the UNITED STATES.

1933 - Commander in Chief Franklin Roosevelt takes office and issues his Executive Order of March 5, 1933 demanding that the Citizens of the UNITED STATES exchange all their gold for paper, Federal Reserve Notes, so we the people obediently surrendered all of our gold. Why? Were we UNITED STATES Citizens? No! We were a sovereign people at that time. We just *assumed* that we were required to turn in all our gold. Whereas only the people living and working in the District of Columbia (Washington, D.C.) and the new 14th Amendment Citizens were required to do so. We were still sovereign at that time. *We were not under the jurisdiction of the UNITED STATES that was incorporated in England in 1871.*

By turning in our gold, we unknowingly *volunteered* into the jurisdiction of the ten-square-mile District of Columbia (*Washington, D.C.*), its laws, and the 14th Amendment.

The Titles to our bodies (*our birth Certificates*) were registered in the Commercial Registry. These Titles to our bodies (*representing our property and future labor*) were mortgaged to the International Bankers as security for the money the UNITED STATES owed the bankruptcy under the authority of commercial Title law.

The American People, themselves, were not in bankruptcy, only the corporate UNITED STATES. Only the ten-square-mile district called Washington, D.C., not the American people.

Artificial Entities

How did we become subjects of the artificial, corporate UNITED STATES? The US CORPORATION has no more power over you than does FEDERAL EXPRESS, *unless that is,* you have *voluntarily* contracted with the artificial entity called the UNITED STATES, in some way.

Well, your mother *unknowingly* pledged your birth certificate to the State when you were born. It was entered into the Commercial Registry to register you as being *"within the UNITED STATES."* This transferred the title to your body to the State via a *constructive, contract trust.* We became members of the *Babylonian System* called the *district UNITED STATES,* in every respect.

Then, the government created an *"artificial person"* — an artificial-entity-strawman — to represent you and to keep you in your place.

Then, via an *adhesion contract,* the government made you a *fiduciary and surety, a co-signer* for your artificial-entity-strawman, to *secure* the National Debt.

By joining together, in partnership with your strawman, you too became a 14th Amendment Citizen of the district UNITED STATES.

All licenses and other existing contracts are made between the UNITED STATES, or THE STATE OF SO & SO — and your artificial-entity-strawman. That *fictitious* entity silently *binds* you to the UNITED STATES, because they made you — *the real woman or man; via an adhesion contract* — a fiduciary responsible for your 14th Amendment Citizen of the UNITED STATES, artificial-entity-strawman. All this by *presumption* without your knowledge or consent; *which is fraud.*

All of the contracts that you have ever signed include your *tacit agreement* to uphold and obey the laws, rules, and regulations passed by the Congress of the district UNITED STATES, and the district STATE OF SO & SO in which you "reside," and these contracts may be enforced in the courts by law against you.

Bankruptcy Trustee takes Possession of Property

Hence, we can never *own* any property, because the State holds Title to it all. We only *rent* our homes that we think we own. We only have a Certificate of title to the "motor vehicle" we think we own, which *certifies* that its Title is owned by the State.

The State owns the true Title to our homes and our cars,

— and everything else that we thought or think we own.

You married the State via your Marriage license, and your children are Wards of the State. *You* are a Ward of the State, too.

All of this, *including the fruits of your future labor,* is pledged to the bankers as *security* against the unpayable, National Debt. All of this was given to the Secretary of State of each State, who is *an agent of the Trustee of the Bankruptcy, named the Secretary of the Treasury of the UNITED STATES, INC.*

1935 - Our pledge was further confirmed when we applied for a Social Security number, via a *silent* contract, when the Social Security Act was signed into law, in 1935.

States Lose Sovereignty

1933 - Commander in Chief Franklin Roosevelt calls all the Governors into Washington D.C. for a Conference of Governors. This Governor's Conference is the beginning of the States' loss of what sovereignty they had retained.

1944 - With the Buck Act, the States become 14th Amendment Citizens as well. This Act ended the ability of *the de facto States* to protect *the dejure States* from being usurped by the CORPORATE UNITED STATES. The corporate States then went under the jurisdiction of the *District of Columbia United States (Washington, D.C.)* at that time.

The March toward Communism

1946 - The Bretton Woods Agreement creates the United Nations.

1964 - Eighteen years later, the Uniform Commercial Code is adopted by all States, and a number of *other* like laws and Acts are incorporated into this nation. The Uniform Commercial Code becomes the Supreme Law of the Land of the United States of America.

We Loose our Courts in 1976

1976 - Congress takes away all semblance of law or

justice left within our court system. All law today is now *construed, constructed,* and *made up* by the judge in *"his"* or *"her"* courtroom.

Congress took away any control or authority we might have had over the court system. Senate Bill 94-204 deals with the Court system, and Senate Bill 94-381 deals with Public Law. This has been well hidden from us all.

Many going into court often wonder why and how the courts can simply override the laws we put into our paperwork. It's quite simple, now that we know how they do it. They *construe* and *construct,* and *make up* what they want.

A simple word such as *in* changed to *at* as in *at law* or *in law* has a totally different and separate meaning. For example: If you're *in* the river, you are wet, you can swim, etc. But if you're *at* the river, you might enjoy a refreshing picnic, play baseball, or run races. See the difference a simple word-change can make? And attorneys *often* change this word when they answer your motions – and also many *other* words as well.

It will pay you dividends to read the answers of attorneys to your paperwork. Compare what they say Case law says, to the actual Case law itself. You'll discover that they have actually changed the words therein. Isn't this illegal, you might say? No! Not according to the above Senate Bills that permit them to **construe** and **construct** what they want.

They can now **construe** and **construct** any law or statute to mean whatever they decide it means, *for their benefit,* not yours. You don't know any of this. You think they are railroading you in a Kangaroo court. No! They are "legal" in whatever they do. They follow the letter of the law, to the letter of the law; *Their* law. Their *private* law. The law of Contract. Contracts that you know nothing about; *Contract law.*

If you don't understand the above and realize what law

you are dealing with when you go into court, you will lose.

Contracts

Even if you have filed your UCC-1 security statement and have captured the Title to your artificial-entity-strawman, it makes no difference, in the above courts. Why? They operate in *total fiction;* in the *La La Land* of Oz. They can only recognize *Contracts,* whereas you are a real sentient being — but with numerous adhesion contracts adhered to you. Whatever you file in their court — whether it is your UCC-1 security statement, or Law from the judicial and original jurisdiction side that is lawful and true — this they cannot see. *They can only see the fictions of Contract law.*

So if you go into any court, be aware that it is a court of *private* law, and the judge and the prosecutor can **construe** and **construct** their law in any way they choose. It will always mean *what they choose it to mean* because you are a Ward of the Court.

So, are the courts bound by the Constitution? By Law? By Statutes? No! **Contracts only** ; and the statutes that enforce *Contracts.* And when we use their statutes, UCC rules and regulations (*all copyrighted*) without a license to practice Law obtained from the BAR, we infringe on their *copyrights,* for which *punishment* of such infringement is mandatory.

There *is no common law* in this nation, nor in the world. There is only *Contract law.*

Summary of Lesson 6.

Throughout history, Babylon, Commerce, and Merchant Law have followed us, wherever we go.

The Bankers were waiting in the wings when we founded this country. The Bankers threw us into bankruptcy, only two years after the Constitution was enacted. The newly founded government moved into the ten-square-mile district that Congress totally controls.

Connect The Dots And See! 57

In 1861, the Southern states walked out of Congress. This officially ended the *lawful* side of the Constitution.

In 1871, the ten-square-miles and the territories that Congress controls were incorporated in England and the Constitution was adopted as that Corporation's By-Laws. This ended the United States Constitution we think of as Law today.

We no longer have a Constitution. We no longer have the protections of the original Constitution and the Bill of Rights, except as a *masquerade* to maintain the peace as the International Bankers tighten their control still more.

The UNITED STATES is a Corporation incorporated by England in 1871, and is under the jurisdiction of England. This entitles England to create laws that the Bank of England and the International Bankers dictate, and every 14th Amendment Citizen is subject to obey those laws. This places the Congress of the UNITED STATES *above* that portion of what we think of as the Constitution of these United States, not under its authority; it is *copyrighted,* remember. The only federal Constitution left at this time are these four Amendments — the 13th, 14th, 15th, and 16th Amendments. These are all the judges are required to take cognizance of and recognize when you appear in their courts today.

Then the *Merchants of Babylon* (*the Bankers*) moved deeper into our Nation by establishing the Federal Reserve Bank, in 1913, and its Collection arm, the IRS, to collect the interest on the loans they make to provide currency for the "for-profit" Corporation called the UNITED STATES.

The 1929 stock market crash, and the Great Depression that followed, placed the American people in desperation, homelessness, poverty and starvation. The minds of the people were focused on survival. They were trapped in a dilemma that forced them to accept any handout the government offered, no matter the cost to their freedoms.

Franklin Delano Roosevelt treasonously placed this entire nation into socialism.

We were drawn in, as 14th Amendment Citizens, through the registration of our Birth certificates. We were further enticed, deeper into that system by *volunteering* for many other licenses and privileges offered by the government, and were made enemies of the UNITED STATES. The 14th Amendment gives the UNITED STATES *authority* over us as a captured people, under the Laws of War, to force *anything* on us they choose to create.

Thereafter, we sank further into Communism. This nation has fulfilled *every* plank of the *ten planks of the Communist Manifesto,* with success. The UNITED STATES is a Communist nation, now. Get used to it; it may never go away.

Then in 1976, Congress removed any semblance of justice in our court system with Senate bills 94-201 and 94-381. From this point forward, the officers of the court **construe** and **construct** the laws to mean anything they choose them to mean.

As 14th Amendment Citizens, we are not citizens of the America we have always thought we knew. We are Citizens of England, through the corporate UNITED STATES.

There is no law today, except a fiction of copyrighted regulations and statutes interpreted by judges who **construe** and **construct** their own private law.

New Beginning Study Course

7
Titles Of Nobility

Almost anyone who has read the *Original* 13th Amendment to the Constitution thinks that this Amendment relates only to Attorneys. This is *mostly* true. However, there are *other* far-reaching and significant meanings to the term "Titles of Nobility."

Title: - *A notice put over, upon, or under anything to distinguish it, or explain it; That which is inscribed; a document, as a Title deed or Certificate; An appellation of dignity, distinction, or preeminence (hereditary or acquired), given to persons by virtue of rank, office, achievement, or privilege; or as a mark of respect. Title may be classified as those of:*

Group A. *Sovereignty attached to hereditary rank and office, grouped in levels such as:*
*(1) **Higher** - Emperor, Tsar, Kaiser, King, Sultan, Shah, Mikado . . .*
*(2) **Lower** - Grand Duke, Duke, Prince. Nobility, attached to hereditary rank, irrespective of office . . .*

Group B. *grouped as:*
*(1) **Greater** – Prince, Duke, Marquis, Count, Earl, Viscount, Baron;*
*(2) **Lesser** – Baron, Knight, Chevalier, Ritter, Caballero, Esquire , Noble.*

(Webster's New International Dictionary 1943).

Nobility: - *Possessing the power of transmitting by inheritance some acknowledged, preeminence founded on hereditary succession; of high birth or exalted rank or* *station, whether inherited or conferred; Quality of possessing characteristics or properties of a very high or order; superiority in excellence, value or the like.*

Attorney

Attorn: - *To turn or transfer homage and service from one Lord to another; to render homage and service to a Lord."*

Attorney: - *To transfer; to turn. One who is appointed or admitted in the place of another to transact any business for him.*

In *our* case, Attorney means to transfer homage and service from our Republic to allegiance to the Crown in England; to the *private* laws of the Bankers and the IMF, to whom the corporate UNITED STATES owes vast sums of money; under whom the corporate UNITED STATES went bankrupt in 1933.

American Jurisprudence defines Attorney

Attorney: - *With obligation to the courts and to the public, not to the client, and wherever the duties of his client conflict with those he owes as an officer of the court, in the administration of justice, the former must yield to the later. — Corpus Juris Secundum, 1980, section 4, See note.*

Note: *By definition, the obligations and duties of attorneys extend to the court and the "public" (read government) before any mere "Client." Clients are "Wards of the court" and therefore "Persons of unsound mind." — See also 'client', 'wards of court'.*

All attorneys owe their allegiance, first to the *Crown of England*, next to the *courts*, and then to the *public*, and lastly to their *clients*. Is it any wonder that your attorney never wins a case for you?

It is the job of attorneys to transfer all our wealth and substance into the hands of the Bankruptcy, for a debt we the People do not owe. *That is their job.* That is their pledge to those to whom they owe allegiance.

BAR: - *British Accreditation Regency.*

Attorneys are members of the BAR. The American Bar Association is a branch of the Bar Council, which is the only bar association, in England. All laws, *today in America,* are copyrighted property of a British Company, all state Codes are private, commercial, British-owned "Law." All Attorneys follow instruction from England.

Attorneys are responsible for following orders from the Crown in England, by drawing up the laws and Acts which brought this country into Bankruptcy. They then, created Titles of Nobility, in various ways, through laws, Acts and Legislation.

All laws, Rules and Regulations for every City, County, State and National government are created by Attorneys in Chicago, on orders from England, which are then sent to the various legislators, city councils and county supervisors across the nation, for enactment. Rarely, if ever, are these Laws, Rules and Regulations read by those who enact them. Most of those people, elected for office, who enact those laws are Attorneys themselves.

The 13th Amendment/Titles of Nobility

The Resolution proposing an amendment to the Constitution of the United States and the 13th Amendment is as follows:

Resolved by the Senate and House of Representatives of the United States of America in Congress assembled, two thirds of both houses concurring; That the following section be submitted to the legislatures of the several states, which, when ratified by the legislature of three fourths of the States, shall be valid and binding, as part of the Constitution of the United States.

If any citizen of the United States shall accept, claim, receive or retain any title of Nobility or honor, or shall without the consent of Congress, accept and retain any present, pension, office or emolument of any kind, whatever, from any Emperor, King, Prince or Foreign power, such person shall cease to be a Citizen of the United States, and shall be incapable of holding any office of trust or profit under them, or either of them.

The War of 1812 served several purposes. It delayed the passage of the 13th Amendment by Virginia, allowed the British to destroy the evidence of the first 12 States that had already ratified this Amendment, and it increased the National Debt, which coerced the Congress to reestablish the National Bank Charter in 1816, after the Treaty of Ghent was ratified by the Senate, in 1815.

Article VI, of The Articles of Confederation, states:

Nor shall the united States in Congress assembled, or any of them, grant any title of nobility.

Article 1, section 9, clause 7, of the Constitution for the united States, states:

No Title of Nobility shall be granted by the united States, and no person holding office of profit or trust under them, shall, without the Consent of Congress, accept any Present, Emolument, Office, or Title, of any kind whatever, from any King, Prince or Foreign state.

Also, Section, 10 clause 1, states:

No state shall enter into any Treaty, Alliance, or Confederation; grant Letters of Marque or Reprisal; coin money; emit Bills of Credit; make any thing but gold and silver Coin a Tender in Payment of Debts; pass any Bill of Attainder, ex post facto law, or law impairing the Obligation of Contracts; or grant any Title of Nobility.

There was, however, *no measurable PENALTY for a violation of the above sections.* Congress saw this as a great threat to the freedom of Americans and our Republican form of government. In January 1810, Senator Reed proposed the 13th Amendment, and on April 26, 1810 it was passed by the Senate, 26 to 1 (*First session, page 670*) and by the House, 87 to 3, on May 1, 1810 (*Second session, page 2050*) and submitted to the seventeen states for ratification.

Enter The War of 1812
The Original 13th Amendment kept Attorneys and anyone with a Title of Nobility from any public office in America. Why was it so important to American Sovereigns to have this Amendment in effect? And what advantage would the foreign Bankers have over American Sovereigns, if this Amendment was *not* in effect?

By 1812, all States had ratified the 13th Amendment except for Virginia. Virginia *did* ratify the Amendment in 1818, after the War of 1812.

Note that the War of 1812 was waged mostly in Washington, D.C. The British burned all the repository buildings, attempting to destroy all records of the new UNITED STATES.

The war of 1812 was partly waged to prevent the passage and enforcement of the new 13th Amendment. Most book repositories throughout the States were burned to the ground and all records destroyed. There's a famous painting in Washington D.C. (*which can be found in many books*) depicting the British boarding a ship after they "surrendered." The painting shows the British soldiers carrying their rifles as they mounted the gangplank to the ship. One might ask, *"What army is allowed to keep their weapons after they surrender?"* One might *also* ask, *"Who really won that war?"*

As a result of the accumulated debt of waging that war, a *new* Bank Charter was issued for another 20 years.

The 13th Amendment was finally ratified by Virginia, the only remaining State necessary to complete Ratification, after the War of 1812, and thereafter became Law.

The Rest of the Story regarding "Titles of Nobility"

In another book we explain the Hierarchy of authority, from the sovereign, to his family, to his neighborhood, to his township, to his county, to his state, to his country, and finally to the planet. Is everything running according to this line of command in today's society? Not quite!

The foreign Bankers knew that they could not control Sovereigns with their system we had so they decided to design a *fictional* system that looks like the real thing *but really is not.*

The first thing the authorities did was to construct an artificial entity which looked and sounded like the federal Republic, the "united States of America." Notice that the "u" in united is a small "u" — that's because it is an *adjective* describing the States (*nouns*) of America. What if one capitalized the "U" as in *United* States? This would be a *name* instead of an *adjective*. It would be a *title*.

So, now we have a *title* for the *democracy* that was incorporated in England, in 1871, as an English corporation. Does this mean that we are being ruled by a *private, foreign* corporation, instead of a government? Yes! Indeed it does!

In 1944, the Buck Act took the Sovereignty away from the States so that the States could *also* have a ***title,*** and ***I.D.*** as in "The State of Idaho" — or ME, as in "The State of Maine." Then came the Counties and Municipalities. Each entity formed their *own* Corporation, which usurped the organic government. What we *now* have is an *inverse relationship* to the original, organic Republics.

On March 9, 1933, The House *(73ʳᵈ Congress, Session I. Chapter I, page # 83, 1ˢᵗ paragraph, 3rd sentence)* stated:

*Under **the new law** the money is issued to the banks in return for Government obligations, bills of exchange, drafts, notes, trade acceptances, and banker's acceptances. **The money will be** worth 100 cents on the dollar, because it is **backed by the credit of the nation. It will represent a** mortgage **on all the homes and other property of all the people in the nation.** (Emphasis added).*

8
Freedom Today

Whenever a farmer finances his farm through a bank or through a farm equipment company — *say he buys a John Deere tractor for example* — he is then tied to the banks jurisdiction, and the bank dictates to him in various ways. The farmer must buy his crop seeds from one of the major seed companies. These companies (*who belong to the bankers or to Standard Oil and the like*) sell only hybrid seed, which means the farmer cannot take a certain portion of his crop and save the seed for next years crops. Hybrid seed will not grow the second year. Plus, hybrid seed requires various fertilizers, which must be purchased from a Corporation. They require pesticides, herbicides etc., all of which must be purchased from the companies belonging to Corporations. Then, the government sets the prices on all products sold. The farmer then must sell only to those same companies *with different names* but owned by Corporations owned by the banks.

Timber was once on land that was *privately* owned, or it was *public* land owned by the people and held in trust *for* the People. During this period, people who owned the land took care not to rape it. They selectively cut the timber by choosing certain trees to be harvested during the year and left the *remaining* trees for the future. Then, all the lands held in trust for the people were transferred to the *Bureau of Land Management* (BLM) and hypothecated by the UNITED STATES to help pay the artificial debt to the International Bankers. Large companies were formed under Standard Oil, and the like, to form companies like Weyerhaeuser, National Paper, etc. who now own millions

Connect The Dots And See!   69

of acres of timberlands. Because of this, these large timber companies wanted to "clear-cut" the lands, strip it clean, which cause all sorts of problems such a erosion and many other harms. It became, and is now, nearly impossible for the private people to buy such lands to harvest the timber. The government does not sell rights to timber in small tracts, such as 1,000 acres, anymore. It now goes into the millions of dollars and prohibits most small business people from entering into the bidding. All the damage done to our forests was not the result of we the People destroying the land, as the Sierra Club wants everyone to believe, it was the huge companies that rape the land, they blame on the little logger.

The same result of the timberlands *also* applies to the mines.

Public Lands are now in the hands of the *Bureau of Land Management* (BLM). You now have to register with the BLM in order to graze cattle on Public Land. It has nearly become so expensive to register and pay the BLM for grazing cattle, that it is prohibitive.

Trademarks, registered with the Patent Office, and bar codes are the means by which the International Bankers track the elements of the world economy.

When you go to the grocery store, all food products are now registered by a bar code.

Can you fly a plane through the air without a license? How about a plane registration and number? How about a radio or television station? Can you still get air for your tires for free at any service station?

Who owns the water rights below the ground in the State of Arizona. It is nearly impossible to drill a water well in Arizona. Even when you can, you must get and pay for a permit.

Can you walk where you want to walk?

When you come to a red light and there is no car in sight,

if you cross against the red light and a cop sees you, what will happen? If you're a smoker, can you smoke where you please? Can you fish? Can you hunt? Can you hike where you want? Can you enter a National Park without charge? Can you burn your barn down if you no longer wanted it? If you have an idea, you must get it patented to protect it. Try building a home of your own design on your own property, do you need a permit?

Money used to be represented by a title called a Gold Certificate. Now a dollar bill is backed by *another* title – *your credit.*

Before you can claim your strawman (*your Title*), you must file a UCC-1 Financing statement and Security Agreement with the Secretary of State of your state. But who can "represent" your strawman-title in a court of fictional law? Not you of course, because you are not a *fiction,* and besides, if you attempted to "represent" your Title in a court of *fiction* you would be using copyrighted material called "statutes," and you could be enjoined in, and charged with the same "crimes" that a *fictitious* Plaintiff is charging the strawman-title with. The strawman-title can't speak for itself because it is a Corporation. So who *can* "represent" your title in court? You said it! An Attorney!

Now, your credit is being *used,* but not by *you.* Fictional laws called "statutes" say you can't. Did you know your "credit" even has a title? It actually has many titles, namely – Federal Reserve Notes. There are many other titles also, including;

a. Federal Reserve Bills
b. Federal Reserve Bonds
c. Checks
d. Bills of Exchange
e. Trade Acceptances
f. Sight Drafts
g. Documentary Drafts

Connect The Dots And See!   71

h. Judgments

i. Any and every bill that you receive.

Spiritual Numbers

In the Bible; *the number 7 = perfection.*

We'll be using the numbers included in the Bible from time to time. We will *also* include a complete paper regarding the meaning of the different numbers contained in the Bible at a later date. But, for now, it will be mentioned that the number 7 equals perfection.

For example, if one goes bankrupt in his private life, how long is the bankruptcy effective? Seven years. Thereafter, in commercial terms, you are purified, perfected and now clean. For a nation, it is *ten times seven* or seventy years.

Now, the first judgment against the United States as a debtor nation occurred in 1788. We could have come out of the Judgment 70 years later in 1858-59. What occurred a few years after *that* period of time? The Civil War.

Now, if we add 70 years to 1859, we get 1929. We know what happened in 1929. Then, if we add 70 years to 1929, we get 1999.

We were *supposed* to come out of *Babylon captivity* in 1859. We didn't. We were *supposed* to come out of captivity in 1929. We didn't. This is what the Commercial Redemption agenda is all about. For those of us who desire to come out of captivity, we have a *window of opportunity* to do so. That's what we are doing now.

Let's again pause a moment in our history. Let's say you have debts beyond your capacity to discharge, or to pay with FRNs (*according to what law form you operate in*) and your debts are overwhelming, you can *file an action* in the bankruptcy court to get relief, or you can *discharge* those debts yourself, because you are in the *bifurcated law form.* There is no *remedy* in bankruptcy court, only *relief,* because you can't *pay* your debts, but you can get *relief* from your debts *by equity credit exchange,* by law.

"By Law" means under the *original* jurisdiction. Look up the words **"lawful"** and **"equity"** in your dictionary, then **"legal"** and compare the difference.

So you go into bankruptcy court and petition, and after a certain amount of court magic the judge awards a *decree of discharge* from the bankruptcy, and your debts are *discharged.*

Now you leave the courtroom after this judgment from the judge. You get out in the hallway and the attorney for the bank, *who holds an unsecured mortgage on your house* says to you, "Excuse me. You still owe my bank client $200,000.00 on your mortgage that was discharged by the court. When are you going to pay up?"

You open your mouth and say, *"Well, I'll try to get them a payment starting next month."* What did you just do to the discharged debt?

You just *reaffirmed the debt* after the discharge. Now that creditor must be paid in full, as it applies to you, and the fact that the bankruptcy court discharged you from that liability five minutes earlier is no longer of force and effect.

All right, let's go back to our history. Let's assume that it was on January 1, 1788, that the United States, as a government, was in default to the Crown of England to the tune of 18,000,000 million Lira, plus interest, and as a result, the corporate UNITED STATES was bankrupt from the start of the United States Constitution. And the debt had to be paid for a period of 70 years.

After the period of 70 years, America could have come out of the bankruptcy with England, on December 31, 1858. (God's Word is *res judicata* and *stare decisis,* meaning **supreme in the eyes of the law**). And let's say, as an operation of law, that some type of Notice was given to the nation that might have gone something like this:

"Excuse me? Do you people really want to leave Babylon and have your liberty back, now, or would you **prefer** to keep the Crown of England as your Master and serve him faithfully?" (*Or something along those lines*).

Look at Deuteronomy 15:16,17 which says, *in effect,* that if you love your master, and your period of service is up, you can go to the judges, recite the fact that you love your master and that you don't want to leave him, and choose to serve him for the rest of your life, and place yourself into "voluntary servitude" to him.

So in the year of 1858, did the Crown of England, through its agent-attorneys, give Notice to the United States? "Hey, you guys want to leave Babylon and go back to the original jurisdiction, or do you want to have your government remain bankrupted under us"?

The Southern States did not wish to remain under slavery to the Crown and walked out of Congress.

The people's failure to give **"Notice of Lawful Protest"** was their tacit (*silent*) vote to remain in Babylon under the Crown of England with continuing debt, plus the reorganized government, because now you are under *a new law forum,* because *the old law forum* was entitled to freedom and liberty. The South walked out, ending the *public* side of the federal Constitution. The people did not protest because they were busy fighting the Civil War, therefore *our officials had to create a* new *law form* that we the People would volunteer into, for another 70 years of captivity.

Original Jurisdiction

You can go to several law dictionaries to look up meanings of law and legal terms. It depends on the author and publisher as to which law forum they publish. If you read *Blacks Law Dictionary* you're going to get *one opinion* of one point of view. If you're reading *Bouvier's or Ballentine's* you might be getting *another* point of view.

Black's Law Dictionary was first published in 1891, 20

years after the corporate United States came into full force and effect by the Act of February 21, 1871. *Black's Law Dictionary* defines the terms and legal meanings of words as they apply to the *bifurcated* United States. There has been a new edition of *Black's Law Dictionary* roughly every 20 years, and if no one gives *Notice of Lawful Protest,* they go on to the *next stage,* and say, "Let's change it again, and see if we can go a little *further,* and see if anybody protests.

So, as we go through the 20 year periods, 1871,1891, 1911, 1931, 1951, 1971, 1991, 2011, we get *different definitions* within Black's Law Dictionary.

Bifurcated means *divided.* The newly incorporated United States is separate from the original jurisdiction of the Republic side under the Constitution. The original Constitution came in with a *private* and *public* side.

The *public* government *can never be changed,* because the government for the *public* is based upon the laws of nature and nature's God, and those laws never change. So the *general* side of government, which we call *Original Jurisdiction,* is based on the laws of nature and nature's God and never changes.

Could you amend the Original Jurisdiction? What would you *amend,* to change that which never changes? It is an oxymoron. So Original Jurisdiction is and *always* remains exactly what it is and it never changes. The law never changes. It is the same yesterday, today and tomorrow.

What is the *other* side, the side that is amended and *does* change? It is *private* government.

Is the *private* government law? No! It comprises the rules that determine the use and applications of the assets and property belonging to the *private government corporation.*

Just think for a minute.

Does a *private* owner of a business or property have

the right to make his own rules, regulations and "law" for the use of his own property? Yes! Indeed, he does. That is *exactly* what the statutes and the regulations and rules are, they are *internal* and they deal with the property and assets of the *private government corporation.*

Did "We the People" fall under the jurisdiction of this *private government corporation* in 1871? No! Only those who lived in Washington. D.C., its territories and 14th Amendment slaves. We were still enforcing the Original Jurisdiction of the Republic and had the authority to do so.

The *original jurisdiction government* was established on certain principles and rules back in 1789, but it went through a *bankruptcy,* almost right away, and with each stage of the bankruptcy there is *reorganization.*

A *reorganization* creates *a new set of circumstances,* and perhaps a new set of creditors or masters or rules to discharge the old bankruptcy.

Roughly, every 20 years you have a *reorganization,* you get different changes in the regulations and rules, and it just goes *on and on,* and the "vise" tightens *more and more* each round.

The proprietors and creditors of that *private law form,* as it goes into stricter and stricter bankruptcy, creating *tighter and tighter* rules in order to raise the revenue to keep the bankruptcy going, and that is what we see happening today.

Do you know now exactly where you are? Do you know what the government has labeled you? Do you know now who you really are?

9
Responsibility

Responsibility: - *To promise in return, answer ; to promise ; to be answerable or liable for creating ; to take ownership of a creation.*

Sounds like a Contract doesn't it? *Responsibility* is an important attribute to have.

We will begin this lesson by presenting words in groupings according to the time-periods that we similarly covered in the previous reports, so that you can see what we have labeled ourselves from the beginning of time to our present day. *Genesis* is where you will find the earliest place in the history of man. Read *Genesis 1:27.*

FIND OUT WHAT YOU HAVE BEEN LABELED

InThe Beginning
Many people call them selves a "man" (or a "woman") or a "flesh and blood man" when writing an affidavit. Please read closely to find out if you really *are* a man, or if that is just a *label* that other sources have put on you, that you have agreed to, without question; without finding the true meaning of the *Word.*

Start reading, *in Genesis 1:27,* about how God made man in his own image.

God created man in his own image, in Genesis 1:27, however, in Gen. 2:5, there was no man to **till** the ground. It appears that there are *two kinds of men.*

Israel goes Into Slavery *Genesis 37)*
This section begins with the story of Israel inhabiting the

Connect The Dots And See!

land then called Caanan (*Merchant*), the future Promised Land where they were *strangers* or *foreigners* in the land.

Joseph was sold into slavery (*by contract*) to the Egyptians by his brothers (*and you were unwittingly sold into slavery by your mother, via your birth certificate*). There are so many similarities in this event that we will compare this story with what is happening today.

Joseph's brothers were jealous of him because of his dreams, so their father made him a coat (*covering*) of many colors (*to conceal his outward show*). But the brothers stripped (*unclothed*) him of the color of law. *Was not this actually a good thing?*

Take out a dollar bill and look on the back of it. Do you see the Egyptian pyramid? This is the symbol and logo of the U.S. Treasury, and the Illuminati. At the top you will see the All-Seeing eye of Horus, the symbol of the Secret Service and the Illuminati. Have you observed the architecture of Washington D.C., with its Egyptian monoliths, columns, stairways and cornices?

What are the *colors* of Egypt? — red, white and blue. What is the *symbol* of Egypt? — the five-pointed star. Egypt means "boxed in." The District of Columbia is ten-miles square.

The District of Columbia (*the for-profit UNITED STATES*) was started by the Illuminati, a Masonic group that originated (*yes*) in Egypt!

What do you think the Illuminati call the UNITED STATES? You guessed it, *New Egypt !*

Joseph eventually was released from slavery and became second in command to Pharaoh. You can go into this event more in detail as it has incredible similarities to current events, but for now we will continue where a famine (*the Great Depression*) is in the land and the remainder of Joseph's family get drawn into Egypt and later into *bondage* – to till Egyptian ground.

In Genesis 5, Pharaoh afflicted the Israelites to the point that they had to gather (*find*) their own straw (*strawman*) in order to make bricks (*transparent, fictional entities*).

Babyon and the Roman Empire

The ancient kings and rulers of the Middle East governed the populace for thousands of years through what they called "city-states" where each city and the surrounding area was a State in and unto itself, independent of the other city-states.

Many conflicts and battles between the city-states took place because of the continual disagreements with the boundary lines between them, in order to keep the people and their land under their control for commerce and taxation. This is where the term "citizen" comes from.

Roman rulers used the term as they conquered each territory by declaring "You are citizens of Rome!" Since the people did not want to fight the Romans, they *acquiesced* and thus they were *verbally contracted* under Roman rule, *as we are today.*

Feudal Titles of Europe

The dark ages brought with it the *feudal society* which appeared to be "new," however, it was the same *enslavement system* but with a new name. There were so many levels and titles of nobility that one got lost in the complexity of it all. We will not go into all of the titles, here, as it would be an entire course in itself, however it is important to define the key titles and levels of serfdom that still linger on, in England and in the UNITED STATES, today, even after a thousand years of custom.

Ask yourself, can a title ever be the *real thing* or is it a *fictional label* with fictitious qualities that can be used to manipulate others?

America, The Land Of The Free (?)

Indentured servants in Europe were frequently offered the option to go to America and work off their debt to the one they owed money to (*and sometimes their life*). Many took the gamble and found that they were able to pay off their debts much easier and faster in the land of opportunity, than they would had stayed in Europe.

Consider the following words:

Trust, trustor, trustee, grant, grantor, legal, description, tenancy, lease, landlord, deed of trust, will, testator, substitutionary executor, fruct and usafruct,

If you think we are no longer in the feudal system here in *the good old US of A.* Think again.

If you, or a friend, have a Mortgage or Deed of Trust, go to your files, and read the first page, and answer the following questions:

1. Did you know that you created a trust when you obtained your house?

2. Who is the *trustor* of the Trust; you or your strawman? — Your strawman.

3. Who is the *trustee* of the Trust? — The Bank.

4. Who is the *beneficiary* of the Trust? — The Federal Reserve.

5. What is the *described property?* The land? Or a list of measurements of a *fictitious location?* — A list of measurements of a *fictitious location.*

6. If you irrevocably "grant" a *legal description* to the trustee, who is the *grantor* and just what exactly was *granted?* — hint: *not the land.*

7. Did the husband and wife sign as *joint tenancy?* If so what does that make the *trustor?* The *owner* or the *tenant?* — The *tenant.*

8. If the *trustor* is now the *tenant* making payments to

the *beneficiary,* is not the bank, in fact, the *landlord* of the property that you think you own? — *Yes!*

9. If one (the mortgage or trust) dies and the property is disposed of - what is it?

10. What really is this document called the Deed of Trust?
   a. a trust
   b. a grant
   c. a lease
   d. a will
   e. a contract
   f. all of the above

11. If you said *"all of the above"* you are correct.

But if the *trustor* is the *strawman,* how do *you* fit into this mystery — are you the *settlor* or the *surety?* — The *surety.*

12. Who gave the *consideration* for this contract?

13. Are the above "persons" and property *real or fictitious?* — *fictitious.*

14. If this is *fiction* - who had the land in the first place before ever walking into the Title Company to sign the loan? — hint: *YOU!*

15. Who is *security* for the Federal Reserve Notes? — same answer: *YOU!*

16. Who then paid for the loan when they signed the Promissory Note? — same answer: *YOU!*

17. So why do we think that we are the *tenant* — when we get a late notice from the bank (*or a Notice of Trustee Sale*) — *when the property was ours in the first place, **and we paid for it with our Promissory Note?*** — *the mortgage contract we signed.*

UNITED STATES: The Corporation

In 1871, the United States was incorporated in England, and became an English corporation under the rule of the Crown (*Rothschild*). As you will see, corporations are not *governments* and can only rule by *contracts* through copyrighted, corporate policy. How can a *corporation* have authority over you?

By silent, or expressed, Contract!

10

Find Out Who You Really Are

Now that you know what you have been labeled (*a strawman*) what did you find? Not a very comforting picture? Well, strap yourselves in. Its going to be a bumpy ride from here on out – *when you learn who you really are!*

InThe Beginning
It is very interesting to see how one can change his viewpoint on a certain subject *after* he defines each and every word on that subject.

It is not our objective here to change your mind, or your life style, or your religion, during these courses, but you will definitely change your point of view towards what you thought were established facts.

Read Genesis 3 in a new light, without preconceived ideas that people have *verbally* told you concerning *the truth*. Then make up your *own* mind as to what the truth is for you.

The positive meaning of *serpent,* is *"to learn by experience; to diligently observe."*

"Be ye therefore wise as serpents, and harmless as doves." — *Matthew 10:16.*

Does this definition of *serpent* differ from the one you have been *verbally* told? Notice: It does *not* say *"satan"* or the *"devil."*

How is your previous definition of **serpent** different from the original Hebrew written over 6,000 years ago?

Connect The Dots And See!   83

You may have been told that the serpent told a lie, but if you read Genesis 3:5, the serpent said something that the Lord later agreed with:

"For God does know in that day you eat thereof, then your eyes shall be opened, and you will be as gods, knowing good and evil."

In verse 22, the Lord states, **"Behold, the man is become as one of us, to know good and evil."** Remember what good and evil are?

Good: - *Good, to make or be good, to please, goods or good things.*

Evil: - *Bad, to spoil, by breaking to pieces, to make or be good for nothing, to displease.*

Good and Evil: - *Increasing and diminishing; going forth and returning; growing a crop and consuming the crop; create and destroy; ebb and flow; to and fro; give and take; up and down; life and death; in and out; pro and con; yin and yang; positive and negative; Light and Dark; God-good and Evil-devil, etc., etc., etc.*

So, did the serpent state a lie or the truth? Does this mean that your definitions of good and evil are not what you thought they were? You are going to have to ask yourself several questions.

1. Is it good to make goods and create things and not be responsible for them?

2. Is it evil to spoil, or consume (*be responsible for*) your goods or whatever you create?

3. Is it even *necessary* to choose between good and evil, or are they *both* essential parts in a complete cycle of understanding?

What is meant by the saying *"if you eat of the fruit of the tree of the knowledge of good and evil, you will surely die"* — was this merely a scare tactic that we gave ourselves to keep us in the status quo? Or is the destruction of our creation an essential step in completing a cycle of action into . . . responsibility? Have you ever heard of the saying *"you can't have your cake and eat it to?"* Well, if you want to believe that, you can, but if I am going to make a cake, I am going to eat it to! This is the mystery of our existence, the evolution of creation, the technology of completion — THE CYCLE OF LIFE — you make your cake and then eat it! Good or bad.

Let's find out more of how Israel got into Egypt (*a box*) by starting with the great grandfather of Israel (*Abraham*) and what his purpose was.

God promised Abraham that he would be *"a father of many nations, and kings shall come out of you."* (*Genesis 17:1-8*).

Jacob (*supplanter*) bought his birthright from his twin brother Esau (*hypocrite*) by trading him a bowl of pottage (*insolence*) when Esau was famished (*starving for the truth*). With the help of his mother (*infinite Mind*), Jacob also got the blessing from his father (*Principal, Soul, Spirit*), which means that he now had the inheritance.

Jacob's name was later changed to Israel and was promised that nations and kings will come from him. (*Genesis 35:10,11*).

Israel multiplies in Canaan until the famine; they then journey to Egypt and find their brother, Joseph, whom his father thought was dead, but who is really alive. This is a similar description of Christ in Revelation 2:8 — *"These things saith the first and the last, which was dead and is alive."*

Israel Comes Out From Egypt

The children of Israel do not become slaves right away; it takes 300 years of a gradual loss of their integrity. Sound familiar? The Egyptian (*hemmed in*) taskmasters afflicted them with increasing burdens (*taxes*) but the Israelites only *multiplied and grew all the more.*

Then Moses is born. Moses was drawn out of the water of the Nile (*river of commerce*) and out of the Red sea (*of confusion and debt*). But first the plagues had to occur, with all their confusion, and death of the Egyptians and their property, before Israel could leave. *Exodus 1-7.*

Remember, the Egyptians worshipped (*created value and worth of*) the river (*commerce*) so when it was turned to blood (*stopped*) they were shocked and dumbfounded and were therefore punished with the value they had put on it. Even the vessels (*weapons, instruments, corporations*) of wood (*firms*) and stone (*buildings*) were filled with blood (*were stopped; became bankrupt*).

There were 10 plagues in all, 10 being a number that signifies law (*the 10 commandments of God's Law*) as in setting forth the law of the administrative procedure (*the 10 maxims of Commercial Law*).

Where do the plagues fit? And where would the plague of the death of the firstborn be? And what does it signify in today's events?

What was the first thing that the UNITED STATES created just after you were born — your strawman. When you claim this entity back from the U.S., "you take it from the Egyptians" and, in their viewpoint, you have killed it because it is no longer subject to their control.

During the plague of the Frogs, plague #4, God put a "division" between Israel and the Egyptians.

There was a "Passover" of the Israelite's firstborn, because they killed, or "redeemed," the lamb by their own will, and put the blood (*estoppel; to stop*) on the door posts (*the Federal window*) as a "Notice" to the destroyer (*the IRS*) to pass over (*exempt*) them. The Israelites killed (*took responsibility for*) the lamb (*their own creation*) so that God would not have to, and for this responsible act, the Israelites avoided loss.

After the plague of the firstborn, the Egyptians wanted the Israelites out of Egypt; GONE! The Israelites borrowed (*laid charge and gave notice of leave*) from the Egyptians by taking valuable jewels of gold and silver (*commercial instruments as valuable as gold, such as administrative procedures and commercial liens*).

The most important point of this exiting (*this Exodus*) was that the Egyptians lost most of their commerce when the Israelites left — the Egyptians lost their power to make money and fill treasuries. What would happen to the world if no one wrote their *credit signature* on another instrument? Today's commerce would completely fold (*your name is your bond*).

The Israelites could have gone out by way of the land of the Philistines (*to their North*), but God said that the Israelites might return to Egypt if they saw war (*controversy*). So they went across the Red Sea by rank of five into the wilderness. As soon as the Israelites walked across the Red Sea on dry ground, Pharaoh's army followed after them and was swallowed by the overwash of the sea and destroyed.

The Israelites journeyed to Mt. Sinai in the wilderness where God gave them the 10 commandments and other judgements and laws. They *also* made the tabernacle for the ark of the covenant. This took approximately one year. Then they journeyed to the Promised Land, where the land was flowing with milk and honey, but when they heard that there were giants and walled cities there, the people said, ***"would God that we had died in the wilderness! Were*** *it not better for us to return to Egypt?"* God *accepted* this murmuring and said, *"as you have spoken in my ears, so will I do to you: Doubtless you shall not come into the land."*

Out of their own mouth was their judgment — duplication of what was said! ("As a man thinketh in his heart..."). The Israelites could not go into the Promised Land (*your goal is contract*) until every last one of the murmurers (*your doubtful thoughts*) died (*vanished*) in the wilderness (*they were subdued by command*), except for Caleb and Joshua who wanted to go in and take the land at that time. After 40 years the Israelites crossed Jordan (*again on dry land*), and went into the Promised Land (*their demonstration*).

The spiritual moral of the story is this: *Out of your own mouth shall come your judgment and fate, you speak* (think) *to your advantage, or to your detriment —* your *choice* creates your reality.

Babyon And The God-Kings
Babylon, Greece, Persia and Assyria, as well as the earlier civilizations Sumer and Akkadia, ruled the populace with an iron fist. In the previous lessons on Commerce you got a viewpoint of what it was like to be a citizen, now you can see the viewpoint of a ruler and the nations that they ruled.

Monarchy Rules!
As you learned, *"it is futile to be feudal",* and, *"it's good to be the king."* What is it like to be a king? The first step is to define what a king is so that you can start acting and thinking and talking like a king. (*An Emissary of God*).

Consider the following words *including their derivations*; king, monarch, royal, roy, rex, lord, loaf, mind, supreme, dominion, master, baron, duke, sovereign

Look up the word *sovereign* in several dictionaries. Look for the definitions that fit what the Americans had in mind when they wrote the **Declaration of Independence.**

In the "Consolidated Webster Encyclopedic Dictionary" of 1939, the derivation of the word *sovereign* is as follows: *souverain,* from *superanus; super; above; over.* The English purposely added the *"g"* in *sovereign* so that it would include the word *"reign"*! The word was also spelled *"sovran"* where the *"e"* has been dropped (*Miriam Webster's Collegiate Dictionary, Tenth Edition*). In the Random House College Dictionary (1984) the word has been further broken down.

My conclusion is that the word *"sovereign"* has been wrongly influenced by the English derivation, and the *true root definition* means *"over and above,"* and that the word should be spelled *"soveran"* (*sov-e-ran*) not *sovereign* and not *sovran.*

So, I am making a big leap here by *declaring "soveran"* *to be an American word,* and that we can spell our words the way we want to, and use them to communicate what we want to communicate.

Soveran: - *over and above; having supreme authority; dominion; rule, rank or power over; beyond jurisdiction; independent and self-governing; autonomous; potent and unlimited in extent.*

Can a *"Soveran"* be under any laws, statutes, or "other authority than God"? No. *A "Soveran" is bound only to what he has said; only to his own words.*

If a *"Soveran"* says that he is under a law or authority — then of course, he is under the very authority of which he speaks.

You may be saying to yourself *"this is too simple, it can't work this simply!"*

All I have to say is — fine! Have it your way!

You can have it however you like because the choice is yours. You are the *"Soveran"*.

You speak your own *circumstance*.

11

America: Land Of The "Soveran"

Hierarchy of Authority

Each of us was born free. Each of us was born a *soveran* being. As a *soveran*, there is a hierarchy of authority in the political arena.

As a man, or woman, you are a king, or a queen. You are *the highest authority under God.* All power rests with you. All lawful authority stems from you. Your only law is the *Golden Rule:*

Never infringe upon the rights of another. Abide by the agreements you *knowingly* make.

You might team up with another and form a marriage, a partnership. A king and a queen may join together and begin a family.

The family unit.

In a family setting, the father has the ultimate authority. He is responsible for the welfare of the entire family. Still, each member of the family is a *soveran* in his own right. So father and mother usually share in the responsibility of rearing the children. Together they establish rules and responsibilities for each of the children to follow.

Never establish harsh punishments and rules. Each child is also a *soveran* as well, but rules and responsibilities teach children the meaning of sharing together with the rest of the family as a team, their responsibility within the family unit, and in life as well.

Neighborhood

Next, come groups of people in your neighborhood. Each father in the neighborhood is the ultimate authority of his family. You can come together as a group for the benefit of all concerned. For example; each neighbor could agree to assist his neighbor if his house or barn caught fire, or if some other such disaster occurred.

However, if you choose not to participate in such an agreement, no one could pass a law or a penalty and enforce it against you. But, it would benefit *everyone* in the neighborhood if you did agree to assist each other.

So, groups of people in a given area are next in the hierarchy of authority. Could people in another state pass laws or agreements for this group of people? Of course not. Even if they did, no one would be obligated to obey such laws or agreements.

Townships

In 1803, President Thomas Jefferson, appointed Lewis and Clark to explore and map out the newly acquired Louisiana Purchase from France — nearly one-third the total area of the United States.

From this endeavor the entire area of the United States was mapped with metes and bounds. We measure, today, boundaries for each piece of property with metes and bounds.

Townships were formed across the nation for every six miles on a side, containing thirty-six square miles. These Townships exist today.

Townships are the next in the hierarchy of power. People within these Townships began to cooperate with each other and towns began to grow. Small governments developed in these Townships so that everyone could better benefit from cooperation with each other.

Still, this *small government* could not, under any circumstances, apply laws that would infringe upon the soveran people. The people were still king and controlled the members of that government.

Counties

County governments are next in the hierarchy of power in politics.

States

The states then created the Federal government called the united States of America. America was a Republic. The Constitution of every State and the U.S. Constitution for the United States guaranteed every State a Republican form of Government. Rule by the People; not a Democracy. (Rule by the Commander in Chief of the military).

Only the ten miles square of Washington, D.C. was to be a Democracy.

In 1776, the Declaration of Independence was signed by the various groups and states and sent to England. England considered the various States their domain to be taxed, to pass laws and agreements for them without their consent or agreement.

The Declaration of Independence gave Notice to the World that all Americans were sovereign People, in which independent and supreme power and authority is vested; a chief ruler collectively, with supreme authority; a king. Thus, We the sovereign People, created the various States, that in turn created the united States of America. *The ultimate power rested with the People.* The Revolutionary War was waged and supposedly won by America.

The soveran people then delegated some of their authority to the States to form a government in each state. A Constitution, an agreement between the people and the newly formed state government *was drawn and adopted by each of the various States. Those Constitutions applied only to those in government.* They did not, nor were they ever intended to, apply to the people within the states. The soveran people were still sovereign. *The people were still king, the ultimate authority.* The Constitutions were merely a contractual agreement for those working in government; guidelines within which government officials worked. *If those government officials overreached or broke the bounds of their State Constitution, there were penalties to pay.*

united States of America

The several states then got together and began to draw up *guidelines for a Federal Government.* These were *the Articles of Confederation.* These Articles were never finished because of factions among the wealthy land owners of the new nation. *Some people wanted to be aligned with England.* Their wealth and prosperity were interlocked in English commerce and rule. *Others wanted to completely separate from England.*

Those who favored England found that there was too much opposition to being bound with England. *As a result, those in favor of England, with the aid of English Bankers, did the next best thing for themselves.* They pushed for a Constitution in place of the Articles of Confederation.

The Constitution was completed and established by the wealthy class before the Articles of Confederation could be finished by the common man.

The Constitution was adopted by several states, in 1789. But a few states wanted some protection from the new federal government established by the Elite. It took another two years for the Bill of Rights to be joined with the Constitution in 1891.

The Bill of Rights was to protect those in the federal government, not the people. Those in the ten miles square who were the employees of that government, never the people.

Soverans do not need constitutional protection, they are REAL people who have natural freedom by heritage as Sons and Daughters of God.

Titles Of Nobility

Now that we have the *hierarchy of authority* mapped out, things are running as expected according to the above line of command. Right? No! Not quite!

The foreign bankers knew they would not be able to control soverans with *this* system. So they engineered a *fictional* system to "look" like the real thing — *"that which seemeth to be, but is not."*

The first thing they did was to make an entity which looked and sounded like the Republic, the *federal* "united States of America."

Notice that the "u" in "united" is not capitalized — that is because it is an *adjective,* describing the *noun,* "States of America".

What if one capitalized the "U," — as in United States? This would be a *name,* a "title," would it not? So, now we have a **"title of nobility"** for the Republic, which our Founding Fathers (*Esquires*) incorporated in England, *as an English corporation.*

In 1944, the Buck Act took their sovereignty away from the States, so that the States could also have a **"title of nobility"** as in **"The State of Maine"**, in place of the **Maine Republic**. Then came the Counties and Municipalities — each were given their own "corporation" which replaced the government of original intent. What we then had was an *inverse relationship* to the original organic Republic States — a mirror image, *instead of fact.*

If you hold the original hierarchy of authority up to the image in the mirror it would look like this.

1. soveran - John Henry Doe (location)
2. family
3. neighborhood
4. township
5. county
6. state

7. country
8. world
_____ (mirrored)_____
1. WORLD CORPORATION
2. NATIONAL CORPORATION
4. STATE OF MAINE CORPORATION
5. COUNTY OF CUMBERLAND CORPORATION
6. TOWN OF BRUNSWICK CORPORATION
7. VOTING DISTRICT
8. STRAWMAN - JOHN DOE (POSTAL ADDRESS)

JOHN DOE - Strawman

If you feel like the "government" has authority over you, or rules your life, then you need to look at who you are, because *that* viewpoint is as being a strawman — the fiction *residing* in the fictitious world of corporations.

The "government" can never have authority over you, because *you* are the government! — a soveran. But a corporation such as the UNITED STATES can obtain a *contract* with your strawman (*another corporation*) through *acquiescence, admission by silence,* and *tacit consent.*

Are you the Soveran or the strawman?

UNITED STATES And The Secured Party

Due to the impending bankruptcy, *since the revolutionary war,* the UNITED STATES has been under many bankruptcy re-organizations.

There are *only two groups of people* in the situation that we have today — *creditors* and *debtors.* A creditor is *also* called a Secured Party, because his financial interest is secured — *not able to be taken away by the debtor* — it is unalienable (un *lien-able;* un *alien* able).

Who gave the **consideration** to make the Federal Reserve notes, bills, and bonds otherwise known in today's commerce as *currency* or *"legal tender"?*

The 73rd Congress, of March 9, 1933, said:

"The new currency will be worth 100 cents on the dollar and will represent **the credit** (*credibility; credible promises*) **of the nation.** It will represent a **mortgage** on all the homes and the property of the people of the nation."

This makes you a Creditor of the UNITED STATES!

Since the UNITED STATES received the **benefit** of **the credit that we loaned to it by pledge** — that makes the UNITED STATES the DEBTOR not the CREDITOR.

The Employees of the UNITED STATES know who you are — a CREDITOR. So isn't it time you started acting like one?

New Beginning Study Course

12
Jack & The Bean Stock

Children's fairy tales have an ulterior motive. Think of the fairy tales as *psychological implants* that you are giving to your children so that they will obey the established *powers-that-be*. This is why you tell the story when the child is in a *semi-conscious* state, so it puts the child to sleep thinking *unconsciously* about the story throughout the night, and in an hypnotic state when they wake.

Find the oldest version of **Jack and the Beanstock** (*1800's or earlier*), perhaps on the internet, since the new versions have been deceptively altered.

One *new* version says, **"Fee, Fie, Fo, Fum, I smell the blood of a Runty one."** Perhaps the author wanted to be politically correct, not wanting to degrade someone by calling him *an Englishman*. Or maybe this story has been altered to cover up its true meaning! If you have seen the *made-for-TV movie* of this story, made recently in 2001, it too gives an altered point of view to the original meaning.

Here is what we discovered from the dictionary definitions of words;

Jack: - *James, John. Being the most common Christian name in France, it became synonymous with rustic or clown, a meaning that it also had in England, where it came to be used as a substitute for the common name, John; the Union Flag of Britain made by uniting the crosses of St. George, St. Andrew and St. Patrick. Rustic or clown; a country bumpkin, or commoner. — 1939 Webster's.*

Poor: - *destitute of riches; not having property; needy; having little value or importance, barren; destitute of intellectual merit, wanting in spirit or vigor; impotent.*

Connect The Dots And See!   99

Magic: - *the art of producing effects by superhuman means, as by spiritual beings or the occult.*

Bean: - *a legume used for food; bean-goose: A species of wild goose which winters in Britain; bean-king: The person who presides as king over the Twelfth-night festivities, attaining this dignity through getting the bean buried in the Twelfth night-cake: A large cake into which a bean was often introduced, prepared for the Twelfth-night festivities: The evening of the festival of the Twelve Days of Christmas and the Epiphany: An appearance or a becoming manifest; specifically, a Christian festival celebrated on the sixth day of January in commemoration of the manifestation of the Savior's birth to the Wise Men of the East. SLANG: your mind; the source for ideas and visions. — 1939 Webster's.*

Cake: - *to take the cake; to* **complete the victory***; to surpass.* — *1939 Webster's.*

Stock: - *the stem or trunk of a tree or other plant; the original race or line of a family;* **lineage***; the property which a merchant tradesman, or company has invested in an business; capital invested in some commercial business or enterprise and contributed by individuals jointly; to store or hoard;* **stock-breeder:** - *a person who breeds live stock or domestic animals.*

Cow: - *the general term applied to the female of the bovine genus. The most valuable to man of all the ruminating animals, because of her milk, flesh, hide, etc. ALSO, to depress, keep under, subdue.*

Trade: - *the business of exchanging commodities for other commodities or for money; commerce; traffic; the place where commercial exchange occurs.*

Cast: - *to throw, fling or send; to turn or direct; to decide against at law, to form by pouring liquid into a mold; to compute or calculate.*

Window: - *an opening in the wall of a building for the admission of light or air; suggestive of a window.*

So that we don't get lost in the definitions, lets see what we have thus far.

Jack (*a commoner in England*) is so poor (*lacking in spirit*) that he takes his cow (*state of being subdued*) and trades it for magic beans (*illusions of the mind*). He takes them to his mother (*the Queen of England*) and she casts (*throws*) them out of the house (*House of Lords, or the House of Representatives*) through the window (*the Federal window; the symbol of the "eye" of Horus; the symbol of the US Treasury*) and into the earth (*called America*).

The bean stock (*lineage*) grows-up "overnight" into the air, above the clouds (*concealed; covered*). Jack, being curious where the bean stock may end, climbs up the stock where he discovers a heavenly place.

Let's look up some more words.

Giant: - *a being of extraordinary stature, strength, intellect or powers.*

Giant: - *[Hebrew nephilim] those who fell.*

Giant: - *[Sumerian Annunaki] those who from heaven came down to earth.*

Goose: - *a swimming bird larger than a duck; a silly creature, an unthinking person; a game formerly common in England played with dice on a card divided into small compartments or counters on which a certain goose was figured, referred to as the twelve good rules of the Royal Game of Goose.*

Gold: - *a precious metal of deep yellow color; money; riches; a symbol of what is valuable or much prized.*

Goldsmith: - an artisan who manufactures vessels and ornaments of gold. *(Rothschild).*

Jesus: - *Greek Iesous, from Hebrew Yehoshua (pro-nounced* **yeh-ho-shoo'-ah**), *from two words Yahovah* **to exist** + *yasha* **to be open**, *wide or to free, deliver, get victory; Yahovah is from another word yehudah celebrated, Judah, from yadah to use the hand, to throw, to revere or worship, from a primary word yad a hand;* **the opened one**, *indicating power, means, direction,* **in distinction from the closed one** *- kaph, kaphaph to curve, bow down self.*

Open: - *akin to* **up and over**; *uncover; unseal; free ingress; accessible; free; liberal; not drawn or contracted; not secret or concealed; truthful and candid; laid bare;* **to reveal**.

Since the word "Jesus" is a Greek word that has been changed by the English derivation, I will refer to him here by his original Hebrew name, **"Yehoshua,"** meaning *"to exist as the one who opens or reveals the truth."* Remember when his body died on the cross, the holy veil was rent which let the son of God be **revealed** and **accessible** to all men? **Yehoshua** (*the true idea of God*) *also* opened the seven seals in Revelation.

Blasphemy: - *blasphemia - vilification, scurrilous, calumnious, impious; from blapto - to hinder, to injure, hurt.*

"Many good works have I shown you from my Father; for which of those works do you stone me?" — *John 10:31.*

The Jews answered him saying, *"For a good work we stone you not; but for BLASPHEMY; and because that you being a man, make yourself God."*

What is with the mind set of this planet that one is discouraged to the extreme from saying that he has created something and now wants to take responsibility for it?!!

Do we have to live our lives continuing to be the **EFFECT** and not dare to be **CAUSE** — for the fear of **BLASPHEMY**? I refuse this philosophy — I know that **I AM** the cause of and for everything in **MY WORLD,** — don't you?

Have you ever heard of the definition of the "criminal mind"? The criminal mind accuses **another** for what **you yourself** are doing.

Remember ... Your world is a reflection — *the reverse image of your mind.* Is it possible that whoever was accusing Jesus of blasphemy was actually guilty of blasphemy himself — by the reversal of the above statement?

"You being a god, make yourself man."

Since we really are Kings and Priests in the sight of God, possibly the ultimate game we created was *so good,* that we believed *it was real* and we created machinery, mechanisms, circuits, and *artificial entities* with *artificial intelligence* to make things **"easier,"** to think *for* us and let them control us more and more so that we eventually forgot who we really are!

Morpheus describes the real world:

"We marveled at our own magnificence as we gave birth to **Artificial Intelligence**, a singular consciousness that spawned an entire race of machines. We know that it was *us* who scorched the sky. At the time, they were dependent on solar power and it was believed that they would not be able to survive without an unlimited resource such as the sun. Throughout human history, we have depended on the **machines** to survive. Fate, it seems, is not without a sense of irony."

So here we are, at the beginning of the lesson course again; at RESPONSIBILITY!

We have come FULL CIRCLE. We started with Responsibility, meaning **betroth** and we end up on the subject of **marriage**.

Responsibility is everywhere you "turn"! But most of our lives we have been running from it; "attempting" to escape from Responsibility.

It is *impossible* not to look, so we must confront our *own* lives at some point. We will have to keep the promise we made in our contract at the beginning of the game we began to play long ago. We will have to take responsibility; and *marry* the *creation* that we have created, to bring it into *fruition.*

Morpheus: I'm only trying to free your mind, *but I can only show you the door* — you are **the one** who has to walk through it. You have to let it all go — *fear, doubt and disbelief* — FREE YOUR MIND! (*Let your* mind become Mind*).

What are the attributes of the number "one"? — *creator, source, originator.*

What are the attributes of "East" — *the front place, the fore part, time, antiquity,* **to project oneself***.*

Some of you have heard about "Commercial Redemption" and the "UCC" (The Uniform Commercial Code).

Some of you are already UCC -1 Redemptors.

Well, what are you waiting for? START TO REDEEM !!!

Genesis 1:

1 *"In the beginning God (source) created the heaven (mind) and the earth (creation)."*

2 *"And the earth was without form and void (confusion) and darkness (ignorance) was upon the face of the deep (artificial basis). And the Spirit (command) of God moved upon (over) the face of the waters (unstable creation)."*

3 *"And God said (commanded), Let there be light: and there was light (duplication)."*

4 *"And God saw the light (understanding), that it was good: and God divided (digested, organized in one's mind) the light from the darkness."*

5 *"And God called the light Day (the sun), and the darkness he called Night (the moon). And the evening and the morning were the first day (cycle of action, circle of completion, age)."*

New Beginning Study Course

14

The Hierarchy Of Law

1. Natural Law
The first order of law on this planet is **Natural Law.**
Universal Principle which so necessarily agrees with nature and the state of man, that without observing their inherent maxims, the peace and happiness of society can not be preserved. Knowledge of natural law may be attained merely by the light of reason, from the facts of their essential agreeableness with the constitution of human nature. Natural Law exists regardless of whether it is enacted positively or not.

2. Commercial Law
The second order of law on this planet is **Commercial Law:** the Law of Commerce.

This most fundamental law of all human law has to do with the universal Principle of Survival. It has to do with human interactions of any kind, any relationship, buying, selling or trading; or relating to others in any way.

Commercail Law based upon treating or dealing with others in the way that you would like to be dealt with, or treated, called **The Golden Rule.**

Commercial Law has been in operation since mankind interacted with each other, begining thousands of years ago in the Sumerian/Babylonian era, where it was codified and enforced.

Ancient artifacts dating more than 6,000 years old reveal that the system was so complex at this time, it even included receipts, coined money, shopping lists, manifestos, and a postal system with the medium in baked clay.

3. Common Law

The third order of law on this planet is **Common Law,** a derivative of Commercial law and therefore the lesser of the two. Common Law (*common; co = together + munis = service, gift; exchange; to exchange together*).

Common Law emerged in England out of disputes over portions of the earth held in *allodium* (*sovereign ownership of land*) and was **based on common sense.**
Common law is the law of the land.

Common law gave rise to the jury system, and the many writs and processes which governments absorbed, statutized into rules and regulations, and the regulatory procedures of the courts.

The procedures of Common Law were based on the necessity *to face your accuser - the alleged injured party - in front of witnesses,* to sort out and resolve the problem directly face to face.

Common Law was never intended to include the *construance of law* by lawyers, attorneys or judges *construing their own law,* since their Titles of Nobility are all based upon the fictions of *hear-say evidence* which can never be the real thing.

4. Regulatory Law

The fourth order of law on the planet is **Regulatory Law.** The legal (*legislated*) Regulations of the organic republic States.

The only Law that the *States* could create was that law which would *allow commerce to flow more efficiently WITHIN the State.*

The only Law that the *Central government, the united States of America,* could create was that law which would *allow commerce to flow more efficiently BETWEEN the States.*

Legislated regulations were never intended to regulate *the people – the "soverans."*

5. Political Law

The fifth order of law is the copyrighted, *private policy of foreign corporations,* such as **THE UNITED STATES, THE STATE OF**... , **THE COUNTY OF**... , **THE CITY OF**... , etc., *or in other words,* POLITICS.

The purpose of these **municipalities** (*'munus,'* service, gift, exchange + 'capere' to take = to take service and exchange*) is **to govern fictitious corporate entities** such as K-MART, WAL-MART; and JOHN DOE and JANE DOE, or JACK SMITH – **not to regulate real people.**

Remember back when you thought that YOU were JOHN DOE — because that's how it is written on your drivers license?

One of our many problems — when we engage with government and other such fictional elements, in our dealings in the law — is that we have been *conditioned by public education* to interact *on their level,* not ours.

Never have we arisen to the level of the reality, the power, the solidity and *the pre-eminence* of the **"soveran"** that we are.

But now we can function at our level of power.

This is CHECK-MATE. The end of the Game. This is REMEDY.

Commercial Law

The principles, maxims and precepts of **Commercial Law** are the same yesterday, today, and forever. They are unchanging, unchangeable, and eternal. They are expressed in both the Old and New Testaments of the Bible.

Commercial Law, unchanged for thousands of years, is the **underlying basis of all law** on this planet and for governments around the world.

Commercial Law is the **Law of Nations** and of everything upon which human civilization is built. This is why it is so powerful.

When you operate at this level, by these precepts, nothing that is of inferior statute can overturn or change it, or abrogate it, or meddle with it. It remains the fundamental source of authority and power, and functional reality.

The Affidavit
Commerce in everyday life is the vehicle, or glue, that holds, or binds, the corporate body-politic together.

Commerce consists of a mode of interacting, doing business with, or **resolving disputes,** by which all matters are executed under oath, certified on each party's *unlimited (commercial) liability,* by sworn affidavit — *or that which is intended to possess the same effect* — as true, correct, and complete, *and not misleading* — the truth, the whole truth, and nothing but the truth.

Such an **affidavit** is the *application* for a driver's license, or for a bank account, or to vote, or a Notary's "Certification of Copy" form, certifying a document, and a *signature* on nearly every document that the system requires citizens to be obligated to or bound.

Such *means of your signature* is an oath, or *commercial affidavit, executed under penalty of perjury, to be true, correct, and complete.*

In a court setting, *oral testimony* is stated in judicial terms as *orally sworn* to be *"the truth, the whole truth, and nothing but the truth, so help me God."*

In addition to asserting all matters under the solemn oath of unlimited personal, commercial, financial, and legal liability for the validity of each and every statement, the participant must provide *material evidence,* i.e. ledgering or bookkeeping *records* proving the truth, validity, relevance, and verifiability of each and every particular assertion, *to sustain credibility.*

Commerce exists and functions without respect to legal system or courts.

15
Ten Maxims Of Law

There are essentially **ten maxims** of commercial law.

1. <u>The workman is worth of his hire.</u> — *Exodus 20:15; Lev. 19:13; Mat. 10:10; Luke 10:7; II Tim. 2:6.*

Legal maxim: *"It is against equity for the free man not to have the free disposal of his own property."*

2. <u>All are equal under the law</u> — "equality before the law" — *God's Law; Moral and Natural Law.* — *Exodus 21:23-25; Lev. 24: 17-21; Deut. 1;17, 19:21; Mat. 22:36-40; Luke 10:17; Col. 3:25.*

Legal maxim: *"No one is above the law."*

This maxim is founded on both natural and moral law, and is binding on everyone. For someone to say or act as though he is "above the law" is insane. This is the *major insanity in the world* today.

Man continues to live, act, believe in, and form systems, organizations, governments, laws and processes which *presume to supercede or abrogate* natural or moral law.

But, under commercial law, natural and moral law are binding on everyone, and no one can escape commercial law. Commerce, by the law of nations, ought to be common, and not converted into a monopoly for the private gain of the few.

Connect The Dots And See!   127

3. In commerce truth is soverign. — *Exodus 20:16;*
Ps. 117:2; John 8:32; II Cor. 13:8.

> **Legal maxim:** *"To lie is to go against the mind."*

This Maxim is one of the most comforting
Maxims we could have; our foundation for peace
of mind and security and our capacity to win, and
triumph — to get our Remedy in the business
called life.
Truth is sovereign — and the "soveran" tells
only the truth. ***"My word is my bond."***
If truth were *not* sovereign in commerce, *in
all human action and interrelations,* there would
be *no basis* for anything. No basis for law and
order. No basis = no accountability. No standards. No capacity to resolve anything. It would
mean that **"anything goes"** - **"each man for
himself"** - **"nothing matters"** - that is *worse*
than the law of the jungle.

4. Truth is expressed in the form of an Affidavit. —
Lev. 5:4-5; Lev. 6:3-5; Lev. 19:11-13: Num. 30:2; Mat. 5:33;
James 5:12.

> **Legal maxim:** *"An affidavit is a two edged sword;*
> *that cuts both ways."*

An affidavit is your solemn expression of truth.
In commerce, an affidavit must underlay and be
the foundation of any commercial transaction
whatsoever. There can be no valid commercial
transaction without someone putting his neck on
the line and stating, ***"this is true, correct, complete, not meant to mislead."***
Someone has to take responsibility for say-

ing that it is a real situation. It can be called a **True Bill** as they say in the Grand Jury. When you **issue an affidavit** in commerce you get the **power of an affidavit.**

You *also* incur the *liability of the affidavit,* because an affidavit presents a situation where other people might be adversely affected by what you say. Things *change* by your affidavit, *which affect people's lives.*

If what you say in your affidavit is in fact *not true,* then those who are adversely affected can come back at you with *justifiable recourse* because you lied. You have told a lie *as if it were the truth.* People depend on your affidavit and they suffer loss when you lie.

5. An unrebutted affidavit stands as truth in commerce. — *12 Pet. 1:25; Heb. 6:13-15.*

Legal Maxim: *"He who does not deny, admits."*

Claims made in your affidavit, *if not rebutted point for point,* emerge as truth in Commerce.

6. An unrebutted affidavit becomes judgment in commerce. — *Heb. 6:16-17.*

There is nothing left to resolve. Any proceeding in a court, tribunal, or arbitration forum, consists of a contest (*a pistolless duel*) of commercial affidavits wherein the points that remain unrebutted in the end, **stand as truth,** as material facts from which lawful judgment is derived.

7. For any matter to be resolved it must be expressed. — *Heb. 4:16; Phil. 4:6; Eph. 6:19-21.*

Legal Maxim: *"He who fails to assert his rights has none."*

No one is expected to be a mind reader. You must put your position out there. You must state what the issue is, to have some issue to talk about, and resolve.

8. He who leaves the field of battle first loses by defaul.

Legal Maxim: *"He who does not repel a wrong, when and he can, occasions it."*

The primary users of Commercial law, and those who best understand and codified it in Western Civilization are the Jews. This is the *Mosaic Law* that they have relied upon for more than 3,500 years, and is based upon Babylonian commerce. — *Book of Job; Mat. 10:22.*

An affidavit that remains unrebutted, point for point, stands as "truth in commerce" because it has *not* been rebutted, and the contender has left the battlefield.

Governments *allegedly* exist to resolve disputes and confirm the truth; to be s*ubstitutes for the dueling field* and the *battle field* of such disputes. Conflicts of **affidavits of truth** are resolved *peaceably* and *reasonably* instead of by *violence*. People can take their unresolved disputes into court and have them opened up and resolved, instead of *going out, marching ten paces, and turning about to injure or kill.*

9. <u>Sacrifice is the measure of credibility.</u> — "Nothing ventured nothing gained."

Legal Maxim: *"He who bears the burden ought to derive the benefit".*

NO WILLINGNESS TO SACRIFICE = NO LIABILITY, RESPONSIBILITY, AUTHORITY OR MEASURE OF CONVICTION.

A person must **put himself on the line** and assume a position, **take a stand** regarding the matter at hand. One cannot realize *a potential gain* without exposing himself to *a potential loss.* One who is not willing to swear an oath, on his unlimited commercial liability, and claim authority for the truth of his statements, and legitimacy of his actions, has no basis to assert his claims or charges, and forfeits all credibility and right. (*Acts 7, life/death of Stephen*).

10. <u>A claim or lien can be staisfied only by rebuttable affidavit point be point, resolution by jury, or payment of the claim.</u> — *Genesis 2:3; Matthew Four; Revelation.*

Legal Maxim: *"Prove your case, or the accused is absolved".*

In commerce, a lien or claim can only be satisfied in any one of the following **three ways**:

10.1. By someone rebutting your affidavit with an affidavit of his own, point by point, until the matter is resolved as to *whose claims* are correct.

Connect The Dots And See!   131

10.2. Convene a common-law jury concerning a dispute involving a claim of more than $20.00 based on the Seventh Amendment to the Constitution, or use a tribunal of three disinterested parties to confirm judgment.

10.3. Pay the claim.

16

Non-judiciable Law

Commercial Law is *pre-judicial.* It is *timeless.* It is the basic foundation beneath which any government or any government court system can possibly function or exist.

What the courts are doing, and what all governments are ultimately adjudicating and making rules about, are the basic rules of Commercial Law. When you go into court and place your hand on the Bible and say, ***"I swear to tell the truth, the whole truth, and nothing but the truth..."*** you have just verbally sworn a **Commercial Affidavit.**

The conflict between Commercial Affidavits gives the court something to talk about and address, the controversy forms the ***entire basis*** of the court's action, ***in their venue.*** **This is one of the reasons why attorneys *always* create controversy.**

No court and no judge can overturn or disregard or abrogate somebody's Affidavit of Truth.

The only one who has any capacity, or right, or responsibility, or knowledge, to rebut your Affidavit of Truth is the one who is ***adversely affected*** by it. It's his *job,* his *right,* his *responsibility,* his *duty to speak for himself;* to issue his *own* affidavit, because no one can speak it for him.

No one else can know what YOUR truth is or has the *free-will responsibility* to state it. This is YOUR job, YOUR responsibility.

Commercial Law
This term describes the whole body of substantive jurisprudence: *the Uniform Commercial Code* and *the Truth in Lending Act,* which are applicable to the rights and intercourse of all persons engaged in commerce, trade or mer-

cantile pursuits.

Commercial Law is intended to maintain the *commercial harmony, integrity,* and *continuity* of society. Its purpose is **to maintain the peace and dignity of the State.**

Over the millennia these principles have been discovered, through experience, and distilled and codified into the fundamental Ten Maxims of Commercial Law listed above.

There is no legal issue or dispute possible which is not a function of one or more of these ten basic principles. The entirety of world commerce functions in full accord with the Uniform Commercial Code (UCC) — commercial law regarding the corporate UNITED STATES.

How To Calculate Your Damages and Collect

Now, here is another aspect of your affidavits. In Commerce there is the **assessment aspect,** which is "who owes whom," and "what, why, how, and for what reasons;" and there is the **collection aspect.**

The collection aspect is based on international commerce that has existed for more than 6,000 years. Again, this is based on *Jewish Law* and the *Jewish grace period,* which is in units of **three; three days; three weeks; three months.** This is why you get 90-day letters from the IRS.

Commercial processes are *non-judicial.* They are *summary processes* (short, concise, without a jury).

THE IRS creates most of the activity of Commercial Collection, in the entire world. The collection *process* is valid even though the IRS is not *registered* to do business in any State.

Do you understand what you just read?

THE IRS IS NOT REGISTERED TO DO BUSINESS OR PERFORM COMMERCIAL ACTIVITY IN ANY STATE.

So how do they get all the money they get?

ANSWER: because you give it to them without requesting *"proof of claim"* from them, or even questioning if they were *"licensed"* (authorized) to give you offers based on *"arbitrary estimations."*

This is where things get very interesting. The other Phase of these matters is the *assessment phase:*

THE IRS HAS NO VALID ASSESSMENT.

The IRS never has, and never can, and never will issue a valid assessment levy or lien. It's not possible.

In order for the IRS to issue a valid assessment there would have to be paperwork — *a True Bill in Commerce.* There would have to be *sworn Affidavits* by someone that such an assessment is *"true, correct and complete, and not meant to deceive,"* which in commerce is essentially *"the truth, the whole truth and nothing but the truth"* when you get into court.

Nobody in the IRS is going to take *commercial liability* for exposing themselves to a lie and have a chance for people to come back at them with *a True Bill in Commerce,* a true *accounting.* This means that they would have to *set forth the contract* — the foundational instrument with your signature on it — to which you are in default, and list all the wonderful *goods and services* that they have done for you, for which you owe them *tribute;* or a statement of all the *damages* that you have caused them for which you owe them *payment.*

To my knowledge, no one has ever received "goods" or "service" from the IRS, for which they owe money. I personally don't know of *anyone* who has damaged *anybody* in the IRS, that gives the IRS the right to come after us and say that *"you owe us money because you damaged me."* The *assessment* phase in the IRS is non-existent. The *assessment* phase is a complete fraud. **You basically assess yourself!**

This is why these rules of Commercial Law come to our rescue.

"We shall not cease from exploration, and the result of all our exploring will be to arrive at the place at which we began, and know a thing for the first time."
— *T.S. Elliot.*

This is the beginning; and this is the end. This closes the circle on the process.

One reason why the super rich bankers and the super rich people in the world have been able to literally steal the world, and subjugate and plunder it, and bankrupt it, and make chattel property out of most of us; is because *they know and use the rules of Commercial Law, and we don't.*

We don't use the rules of Commercial Law because we don't know the rules. **We don't know what the game is.** Therefore, we don't know what to do. We don't know how to invoke our recourses, remedies, and rights. We get lost in doing everything under the sun except the one and only thing that is the solution.

No one is going to explain to you what and how all this is happening to you. It is never going to happen. **The powers-that-be will *never* divulge the rules of the game.**

They can get away with complete fraud and steal everything because no one knows what to do about it.

Well, what *CAN* you do about it?

You Can Issue A Commercial Affidavit.

You don't have to call it an affidavit but that is what it is. You could assert in your affidavit such claims as these:

"I have never been presented with any sworn affidavits that would provide validity to your assessment. It is my best and considered judgment that no such paperwork or affidavit exists."

At the end of this document, you could put *demands* on

them, and a *time limit* for their response, and that their response must be explicit. The then you state: *"Should you consider my position in error . . ."*

Now, they must respond with an affidavit which rebuts *your* affidavit point for point. This means that they have to provide the paper work with *a real* assessment, a *true bill in commerce,* a real sworn affidavit that would make their assessment or claims against you valid. Such an assessment they do not have.

No agent (*attorney*) of a fictitious entity can sign an affidavit for the corporation. How can they swear as fact that the corporation has done or not done ANYTHING? *They do not have the standing to do so.* They cannot and never will provide you with this. This means your affidavit stands as truth in commerce.

You can even make it more interesting if you like.

You go to all their laws such as U.S. Code Title 18 CRIMES AND CRIMINAL PROCEDURE and tabulate the whole list of crimes they have committed against you in lying to you, foreclosing and selling your home, and issuing liens and levies. This could be quite an impressive list.

If you tabulate the dollar amounts of the fines involved in these offenses, you could take just **Title 18 section 241** *alone* which is a **$10,000.00 fine** on any public official *for each offense.* That means for every single violation of the Constitution, or commercial law, there could be 35 or 40 of these in Title 18. You're looking at $300,000 to $400,000 dollars. When they start adding up, they become very impressive.

Now you attach this *criminal accounting* to your affidavit and you *file it as a criminal complaint with the State Attorney — the Attorney General of the State.* This is like putting the fox in charge of guarding the hen house.

Attach your affidavit and your criminal complaint to a commercial lien. But wait! There is even a more effective way of getting your equity back – Involuntary Bankruptcy!

The reason you go through this criminal complaint is because, *by their own laws and value system and penalties,* they have hung themselves. They have *already* discerned and formulated the dollar amount involved in each of the various offenses. When you *lien* them for those amounts, they can't come back and say: ***"Well, these dollar amounts are out of nowhere. They're unreasonable. Where did you get this?"*** Right out of your own codes.

Commercial Processes Are Non-judicial, Pre-judicial, And Are More Powerful Than The Judicial Processes.

Now, you take your commercial lien to the Secretary of State and file it as a *UCC-1 Financing statement.* Then as soon as you've finished filing the original criminal complaint with the Prosecuting attorney, you file this lien against every public agent individually. *(The criminal complaint is optional).* They can't hide behind the skirts of the *corporate state — the fictional entity created by man so he can engage in perfidious actions which he would not otherwise be able to do according to Natural and Moral Law.* It just doesn't work.

Now, you can use this same collection process against them that the IRS uses against you.

You will discover that all the attorneys, judges and the people who come against you think this is a lot of gobble-di-gook, hogwash, and silly. But they soon learn that *your affidavit of truth* is valid and enforceable against them. And they find that things become more and more uncomfortable with each passing day.

Judges think all this doesn't matter because they can get another judge to remove all your paperwork against them. Other agents of the government think they can hide behind the sovereign immunity of the Government, behind all that power and prestige and all their capacity to get the courts to do whatever they wish is going to save them. None of these have any effect on your process.

It has no effect because *there is only one way that they can be saved and that is to come in with their own affidavit that rebuts your affidavit point by point and proves you wrong.* If they did get this into a court or jury, it won't do them any good because the same battle still exists there.

This would mean that *the conflict between affidavits* is now fought out in the open. And that is embarrassing to them because they are not able to change anything. This will simply do them more harm.

The *third* way for them to resolve and settle your claim is to pay it. If they don't satisfy your claim, you give them a period of grace, *and at the end of 90 days you transform the Secretary of State into your Accounts Receivable Office for collection.* Legal Title of all their real and personal property will have now passed to you. Now, you file the correct paperwork with the Secretary of State, and serve this on the Sheriff and say, *"I want to take possession of my property."* Things then begin to get interesting.

If you send a criminal complaint on a public official to the Insurance Commissioner of the State, it becomes automatically a lien against the bond of the official, the judge or district attorney and he's dead in the water. *He cannot function without bonding.* This is held in suspension until the issue is resolved.

Now, simply by going back to what we've wanted all along, which is *truth, rightness* and a *remedy,* and *finding the rules that pertain to it,* all of a sudden we find that we have more power than they do, since we are sovereign.

No one, not a judge, jury or anyone else can overturn or change this process.

To do so would be to dissolve the world immediately into chaos. This would be the end of all law, all order, all standards, for all civilization.

It is not possible. They are stuck. This is the way to put power on your side and against those agents of government who violate your being, and injure you in violation of their oath of office.

That is how, through their own process, we can use the rules of the game in OUR favor instead of remaining in ignorance and being taken forever as slaves. This applies to everything, not just to the government. This forms a valid foundation for your life and it forms a basis for any kind of your dealings with government. What most people don't realize is that governments don't have, and can't have, anything to support an affidavit of truth that supports their actions when their actions are wrong.

Governments invent all the regulations and statutes they impose on you, affecting your life and commercial/economic standing. And no one is taking any liability, responsibility, nor accountability. They may have some kind of bonding. But in most states this bonding is only for about $5 million to $10 million dollars for the entire state, and all its employees, but you can tabulate a simple traffic ticket into more than $5 million dollars if you choose to do so.

Uniform Commercial Code

The National Conference of Commissioners on Uniform State Laws together with the **American Law Institute** drafted **Nationwide Uniform Laws** and each state has now adopted these laws. **These laws govern commercial transactions,** including sales and leasing of goods, transfer of funds, commercial paper, bank deposits and collections, letters of credit, bulk transfers, warehouse receipts, bills of lading, investment securities, and secured transactions.

"The UCC has been adopted in whole or substan-

tially by all states. " — *Blacks 6ᵗʰ.*

The UCC is a code of laws governing various commercial transactions — sale of goods, banking transactions, secured transactions in personal property, and other matters, that was designed to bring uniformity in these areas to the laws of the various states, and that has been adopted, with some modifications in all states, including the District of Columbia and the Virgin Islands. — *Barron's 3ʳᵈ edition.*

Unless displaced by the particular provisions of this code, the principles of law and equity — *including the law merchant and the law relative to capacity to contract, principal and agent, estoppel, fraud, misrepresentation, duress, coercion, mistake, bankruptcy, or other validating or invalidating cause* — shall supplement its provisions. — *UCC 1-103.*

To paraphrase the third definition above, **the UCC is the supreme law of the land on the planet and all other forms of law are encompassed by it and included in it,** except you and me as soverans, of course.

Pennsylvania was the first state to adopt the UCC, on July, 1954; and Louisiana the last on January, 1975.

The following is a quote from the *Bank Officers Handbook of Commercial Banking Law Within the United States, sixth edition, paragraph 22.01(1)* and pertains to certain types of transactions:

"There are (12) transactions to which the UCC does not apply. They are as follows:

1. Security interests governed by federal statutes;
2. Landlord liens;
3. Liens for services or material provided;
4. Assignment for claims for wages;
5. Transfers by government agencies;
6. Isolated sales of accounts or chattel paper;
7. Insurance Policies;

8. Judgments;
9. Rights of setoff;
10. Real Estate interests;
11. Tort Claims;
12. Bank accounts.

UCC-104, Construction against implicit repeal.
"This code being a general act intended as a unified coverage of its subject matter, no part of it shall be deemed to be impliedly repealed by subsequent legislation and in such construction be reasonably avoided".

Nothing in the UCC has ever been repealed, nor can it ever be.

In the event of conflict between a *deleted* section and a *current* section, the deleted section controls. It cannot be the other way around. Potentially countless commercial transactions can be consummated based on the current UCC, at any time.

To **"cancel"** any portion of the UCC, at a later point, would throw into upheaval and chaos all commercial agreements that were based on the deleted portion, an act that would carry unimaginable, astronomical liability to the many actors who attempted to effect such change.

Now, we must define the United States. This was covered before, but we will define it again, for a better understanding as applied to this procedure at hand.

17
Working With The Law

Commercial Lien

A commercial lien is a *non-judicial* claim or charge against property of a Lien Debtor for payment of a debt or discharge of a duty or obligation. A lien has the effect of permanently seizing property in three months (*ninety days*) upon failure of the lien debtor to rebut the affidavit of Claim of Lien.

The commercial grace of a lien is provided by the three-month delay of the execution process, allowing resolution either verbally, in writing, or by jury trial within the 90 day period of grace.

A **distress** (*defined in Blacks 6th*), bonded by an **affidavit of information,** becomes *a finalized, matured commercial lien and accounts receivable* ninety days from the date of filing. The Lien Right of a lien must be expressed in the form of an *affidavit sworn true, correct and complete, with positive identification of the affiant.* The swearing is based on one's own commercial liability.

A **commercial lien** differs from a **true bill in commerce,** only in that **a true bill in commerce** is ordinarily private whereas a **commercial lien** is a **true bill in commerce publicly declared,** usually filed in the office of the County Recorder, and when uncontested by point for point rebuttal of the affidavit *it becomes a Security per 15 USC, and an accounts-receivable.*

A *commercial* lien differs from a *non-commercial* lien in that it contains a declaration of a one-to-one correspondence concerning an item or service purchased, or offenses committed and a debt owed.

A commercial lien does not require a court process for its establishment. However, *a commercial lien can be chal-*

lenged via a Seventh Amendment jury trial, but may not be removed by anyone except the Lien Claimant, or such jury trial properly constituted, convened, and concluded by due process of law. It cannot be removed by *summary process,* i.e. a judge's discretion.

A commercial lien (or distress) can exist in ordinary commerce without dependence on a judicial process, and is therefore not a common law instrument unless challenged in a court of common law, whereupon it converts to a common law lien.

A commercial lien must *always* contain an **Affidavit in support of Claim of Lien** and cannot be removed without a complete rebuttal of the Lien Claimant's affidavit, point-by-point, in order to overthrow the one-to-one correspondence of the commercial lien.

No common law process can remove a commercial lien unless that common law process guarantees and results in a *complete rebuttal* of the lien claimants Affidavit, categorically and point-for-point, in order to overthrow the one-to-one correspondence of the commercial lien.

What is a True Bill in Commerce?

A True Bill in Commerce is a ledgering or bookkeeping/accounting with every entry established. This is your first Affidavit, certified and sworn on the maker's commercial liability as true, correct, and complete, and not meant to mislead. It must contain a one-to one correspondence between an item or service purchased or offenses committed and the corresponding debt owed.

This commercial relationship is what is known as **"Just compensation"** (*5th Amendment*) between the Government and the American people. A **True Bill** is called a **"warrant"** (*4th Amendment*), and **direct taking of property by legislative act** (*e.g. IRS and the like*) is called a **Bill of Pains and Penalties** (*Constitution, Art. I, Section 10,* *clause l, and Article l, Section 9, clause 3, Bill of Attainder).*

There is one other matter we must define before we start putting all these pieces of the puzzle together into a workable tool for our benefit. That is the Uniform Commercial Code itself.

UNITED STATES, US, U.S., USA, and **AMERICA,** means **"federal corporation."** — *USC Title 28, Section 3002(5), Chapter 176.*

The UNITED STATES is a corporation. — *534 Federal Supplement 724.*

The UNITED STATES is a corporation originally incorporated on February 21, 1871 under the name of the "District of Columbia". — *16 Stat. 419 Chapter 62.*

The UNITED STATES was reorganized June 11, 1878 and is a bankrupt organization per House Joint Resolution 192 on June 5, 1933. — *Senate Report 93-549, and Executive Orders 6072, 6102, and 6246.*

The UNITED STATES is a de facto government, originally the ten square mile tract ceded by Maryland and Virginia, comprising Washington D. C. — and its possessions, territories, arsenals and forts.

As a corporation, the **UNITED STATES** has no more authority to implement its laws against **The People** than does the **MacDonald Corporation**, except for **the *silent* contracts we have signed as surety for our strawman with the UNITED STATES and its Creditor Bankers.** These *silent contracts* (*with the UNITED STATES and the bankers*) are not contracts with us, but with our *artificial entity strawman,* or as they term it, the ***person*** which appears to be us but is printed with the ALL CAPITAL LETTERS that signify a corporation.

All this was accomplished under. . .

Vice-admiralty Courts.

Vice-Admiralty Courts are Courts established in the Queen of England's possessions beyond the seas, having jurisdiction over maritime causes, including those relating to prize.

The United States of America is lawfully a possession of the English Crown per original commercial joint venture agreement between the colonies and the Crown and the Constitution that brought all the States back under British ownership and rule.

The American people, however, had sovereign standing in law *independent* of any connection to the States or the Crown. This fact required that the people be brought back under British Rule, one at a time, and the **"commercial process"** was the method of choice used to accomplish this task, first through the 14th Amendment, then through the registration of our birth certificates and our property with the state. All courts in America are **Vice-admiralty courts** operating in the Crown's private commercial domain.

'Accept For Value And Acceptance'

By now, you have probably heard the term *acceptance for value*. This term was difficult for me to understand when first encountered, and most of the people learning these redemption lessons seem to have the same problem at the start.

When you look up the word **"accept"** in Blacks 4th Edition you find, *"to receive with approval or satisfaction; to receive with specific intent to retain."*

When you get a traffic ticket, a notice of foreclosure, a notice of levy from the IRS — or whatever — one's first instinctive reaction is, *"Oh, No! I'm certainly not going to 'accept' this thing!"* Why would *anyone* want to accept any such thing? Let's look at the words used.

Acceptance: - *the taking and receiving of anything in good part, as a **tacit agreement** to a proceeding part, which might have been defeated, or avoided, if such an acceptance had not been made.*

Nope, that doesn't sound much better, does it?

Tacit: - *existing, inferred, understood without being openly expressed or stated; implied by silence or silent acquiescence, as a tacit agreement or a tacit understanding. Done or made in silence, implied or indicated, but not actually expressed. Manifested by the refraining from contradiction or objection; inferred from the situation and circumstances, in the absence of express matter. — Blacks 6th.*

If I **"accept"** something then there is an agreement. I agree with what they have said in the writing, whatever it may be.

But if I don't **"accept"** it, but fail to **express** my objection, then there is **still** an agreement because I didn't **refute** it or contradict what was said in the writing.

I don't want to get into a court battle with anyone.

No matter how right you might think you are, no matter what law you think is on your side, you will always *lose your **defense*** in any court. Period.

What a predicament.

So, why would I want to **accept** anything **for value?** How could that phrase possibly be of any help to me?

Conditional acceptance: - *An agreement to pay the draft or to accept the offer **on the happening of a condition subsequent*** (meaning after).

A **conditional acceptance** is, in effect, a statement that the **offeree** (*meaning you*) is **willing** to enter into a contract that's different from the offer proposed in the original offer. **A conditional acceptance is a *counter offer.***

OK. That sounds a little better.

If I accept their offer with a **conditional acceptance** I am making a **counter offer** back to them and the ball is now in their court.

If they do not answer within a reasonable period of time, *which I can specify,* then they accept **my** offer by *tacit agreement* — and I win.

This sounds better. But we're not through yet.

Let's look at: **Power of Acceptance**

Power of acceptance: - *the capacity of the offeree (meaning you), upon acceptance of the terms of offer,* **to create a binding contract.** — *Blacks 6th.*

So, if I accept your offer with a conditional acceptance, and specify my own terms on which I *do* accept your offer then I have offered you a binding contract **for you to accept, or reject by proving your claim valid.**

The **offeror** (*a municipality or corporation*) must now come back to you with a rebuttal to prove that your terms and conditions are in error.

You need to **"accept for value"** these silent contracts by claiming **legal possession** of the *fictitious-entity-strawman* that the State created to **represent** (*re-present*) **you** when you were born.

Commercial Redemption

The UNITED STATES defines the fictitious entity spelled like your name with all caps — your strawman — as a "corporation of one" a legal "person" so-called

Corporation: - *any company, trust, or association, incorporated or unincorporated, which is organized to carry*

on business for its own profit or the profit of its members."
— *15 USCA (United States Code Annotated) section 44.*

Since the State created this **"unincorporated corporation"** the State has full authority over it. And unless and until you **object,** and give them notice otherwise, they will always have authority over your strawman, *and through him* over you.

A **UCC-1 Financing Statement** (*declaration*) gives public notice that you, *the secured party, the secured party creditor,* have a *superior claim* against the *debtor,* the unincorporated corporation of one, your strawman.

When you file this Notice (*declaration*), you take this entity **"out of the state"** (*out of the jurisdiction of the fictitious entity State*) into the private domain (*venue*) where you are king. The entity (*your redeemed strawman*) becomes **"foreign to the State"** — your strawman becomes an unincorporated corporation foreign to the State.

Sounds like an oxymoron, but this is **THEIR** terminology and **THEIR** law! We simply *discovered* how it works.

Financing Statement: - *a document setting out a secured party's* **security interest** *in goods. A document designed* **to notify third parties,** *generally prospective buyers or lenders,* **that there may be** *an enforceable security interest in the property of the debtor. It is evidence of* **a security interest filed by the security holder with the Secretary of State,** *or similar public body, that has becomes public record.*

Security Agreement: - *an agreement which creates or provides for a security interest between the debtor and a secured party. UCC-9-105(h). An agreement granting a creditor a security interest in personal property, which security interest is normally perfected either by the creditor taking possession of the collateral or by filing financing statements in the proper public records.*

Security interest: - *interest in property obtained pursuant to security agreement; A form of interest in property which provides that the property may be sold on default in order to satisfy the obligation for which the security interest is given; Often "lien" is used as a synonym, although lien most commonly refers only to interests providing security that are created by operation of law, not through agreement of the debtor and creditor.*

A **security agreement** establishing a security interest must exist in order to file a **UCC-1 Financing Statement** — but does this mean that it must be in writing and attached to the UCC-1?

Perhaps, but not if it is a **verbal agreement.**

Since your strawman corporation cannot speak, how can it write or sign its name? You can create a security agreement, and attach it to your UCC-1 Financing Statement, but you probably don't need it. In fact, you can do all of the administrative procedures without filing a UCC-1 because **you are the Secured Party Creditor whether you file a UCC-1 or not.**

Filing is as much for **your** benefit as for anyone else because it makes this *intangible subject* more real to **you** and gives you confidence, and that alone is worth every bit of the effort expended.

Some of the states give you a hard time when filing the Financing Statement, as they claim you are "contracting with yourself." You can overcome this by creating a separation between you and your strawman corporation so that they can see the difference (*as if they didn't know*).

You could apply for a **tradename** for your strawman--corporation-of-one. Once this is filed, you will start receiving promotions in the mail, indicating that the "corporate system" recognizes your strawman as a **fictitious entity** doing business for profit, as a corporation.

18

Balancing Your Account

Balancing Your Account With The Treasury of The United States

The government — *specifically, the IRS* — keeps an account for your **strawman-corporation** from the time you were born until the time you die. That is what the strawman is – *a ledger account* — an accounting of the commercial transactions of the credit that you *as the creditor* give or loan to the **UNITED STATES**.

The IRS calls the summary of entries made to this account your **Individual Master File** (IMF). This file is an account of what the strawman does, so that they can put a value on the *criminal charges* that they are claiming against your "individual" strawman; such as being a *rum runner in Puerto Rico,* or an *arms dealer in Iran,* or a *drug dealer in Malaysia.*

That is how they *charge against your account* and that is why you have never been "directly" charged with these crimes – the *debtor,* the *corporation,* your *strawman* is charged instead. These "charges" represent millions of dollars worth of U.S. Treasury Bonds sold and traded by the foreign corporation called the UNITED STATES.

As you might guess, depending on the crimes and the assigned values, this balance is a *continuing deficit* to the *debtor,* and it would be an overwhelming feeling to know that — *if you think you are the debtor* — you might owe millions if not hundreds of millions of dollars to someone else.

But you must ask yourself this question, *"who is the creditor of this unredeemed, debtor strawman?"* Is it THE UNITED STATES, THE FEDERAL RESERVE BANK, or THE INTERNATIONAL MONETARY FUND?

No! YOU are the creditor of your debtor strawman, whether redeemed or not. These entities are **pretending** to be the creditors in your place, but did they create the substance (*value*) or did you?

Then why are they getting the *interest* (*taxes*) for the credit units that WE have supplied to the corporations? Shouldn't the corporations be paying the *interest* (*taxes*) to us instead of us to them?

How did this get turned upside down where the head is the tail and the tail is the head?

"The stranger that is within you shall get up above you very high; and you shall come down very low. He shall lend to you and you shall not lend to him; he shall be the head, and you shall be the tail. Moreover all these curses shall come upon you, and shall pursue you, and overtake you, till you be destroyed; because you hearkened not unto the voice of the Lord your God, to keep his commandments and his statutes which he commanded you." — *Deuteronomy 28:43, 44 & 45.*

Now that you can visualize the countless number of "charges" that have been entered by the IRS against your corporate strawman's account, what can you do about it?

You can balance your account by ACCEPTANCE FOR VALUE. You can *redeem* (*zero out*) this account with your credit and you can discharge all of the other debts that you can see in the public domain.

The following is a speech by Representative James Traficant: Report On The Bankruptcy Of the United States, United States Congressional Record, March 1, 1993, VOL.

33, page H-1303. The Speaker - Rep. James Traficant, Jr. (Ohio) - addresses the House.

Mr. Speaker, we are here now in chapter 11 bankruptcy reorganization.

We members of Congress are official trustees presiding over the greatest reorganization of any Bankrupt entity in world history, the U.S. Government. We are setting forth, hopefully, a blueprint for our future. There are some who say it is a coroner's report that will lead to our demise.

It is an established fact that the United States Federal Government has been dissolved by the Emergency Banking Act, March 9, 1933, 48 Stat. 1, Public Law 89-719; declared by President Roosevelt, being bankrupt and insolvent.

HJR 192, 73rd. Congress in session, June 5, 1933 - Joint Resolution To Suspend The Gold Standard and Abrogate The Gold Clause, dissolved the Sovereign Authority of the United States and the official capacities of all United States Government Offices, Officers and Departments, and is further evidence that the United States Federal Government exists today in name only.

The receivers of the United States Bankruptcy are the International Bankers, via the United Nations, the World Bank and the International Monetary Fund. All United States Offices, Officials, and Departments are now operating within a defacto status in name only under Emergency War Powers. With the Constitutional Republican form of Government now dissolved, the receivers of the Bankruptcy have adopted a new form of government for the United States. This new form of government is known as a Democracy, being an established Socialist/Communist order under a new governor for America. This act was instituted and established by transferring and/or placing the Office of the Secretary of Treasury to that of the Governor of the International Monetary Fund. Public Law 94-564, page 8, Section H. R. 13955 reads in part: "The U.S. Secretary of Treasury receives no compensation for representing the United States?"

Gold and silver were such a powerful money during the founding of the United States of America, that the founding fathers declared that only gold and silver coins can be "money" in America. Since gold and silver coinage were heavy and inconvenient for a lot of transactions, they were stored in banks and a claim check was issued as a money substitute. People traded their coupons as money, or "currency." Currency is not money, but a money substitute. Redeemable currency must promise to pay a dollar equivalent in gold or silver money. Federal Reserve Notes (FRN's) make no such promises and are not "money." A Federal Reserve Note is a debt obligation of the federal United States government, not "money." The federal United States government and the U.S. Congress were not and have never been authorized by the Constitution for the United States of America to issue currency of any kind, but only lawful money - gold and silver coin.

It is essential that we comprehend the distinction between real money and a paper money substitute. One cannot get rich by accumulating money substitutes, one can only get deeper in debt. We the People no longer have any "money." Most Americans have not been paid any "money" for a very long time, perhaps not in their entire lifetimes. Now do you comprehend why you feel broke? Now, do you understand why you are "bankrupt," along with the rest of the country?

Federal Reserve Notes (FRN's) are unsigned checks written on a closed account. FRN's are an inflatable paper system designed to create debt through inflation (devaluation of currency). Whenever there is an increase of the supply of a money substitute in the economy without a corresponding increase in the gold and silver backing, inflation occurs.

Inflation is an invisible form of taxation that irresponsible governments inflict on their citizens. The Federal Reserve Bank who controls the supply and movement of FRN's has everybody fooled. They have access to an unlimited supply of FRN's, paying only for the printing costs of what they need. FRN's are nothing more than promissory notes for U.S. Treasury securities (T-Bills) - a promise to pay the debt to the Federal Reserve Bank.

There is a fundamental difference between "paying" and "discharging" a debt. To pay a debt, you must pay with value or substance (i.e. gold, silver, barter or a commodity). With FRN's, you can only discharge a debt. You cannot pay a debt with a debt currency system. You cannot service a debt with a currency that has no backing in value or substance. No contract in common law is valid unless it involves an exchange of "good and valuable consideration." Unpayable debt transfers power and control to the sovereign power structure that has no interest in money, law, equity or justice because they have so much wealth already.

Their lust is for power and control, and since the inception of central banking, they have controlled the fates of nations.

The Federal Reserve System, is based on the Canon law and the principles of sovereignty protected in the Constitution and the Bill of Rights. In fact, the international bankers used a "Canon Law Trust" as their model, adding stock and naming it a "Joint Stock Trust." The U.S. Congress had passed a law making it illegal for any legal "person" to duplicate a "Joint Stock Trust" in 1873. The Federal Reserve Act was legislated post-facto (1870), although post-facto laws are strictly forbidden by the Constitution. (Art. 1, § 9, cl .3)

The Federal Reserve System is a sovereign power structure separate and distinct from the federal United States government. The Federal Reserve is a maritime lender, and/or maritime insurance underwriter to the federal United States operating exclusively under Admiralty/Maritime law. The lender underwriter bears the risks, and the Maritime law compelling specific performance in paying the interest, or premiums are the same.

Assets of the debtor can also be hypothecated as a security (to pledge something as a security without taking possession of it) by the lender or underwriter.

The Federal Reserve Act stipulated that the interest on the debt was to be paid in gold. There was no stipulation in the Federal Reserve Act for ever paying the principal.

Prior to 1913, most Americans owned clear, allodial title to property, free and clear of any liens or mortgages until Federal Reserve Act (1913) "hypothecated" all property within the federal United States to the Board of Governors of the Federal Reserve, in which the Trustees (stockholders) held legal title, the U.S. citizen (tenant, franchisee) was registered as a "beneficiary" of the trust via his/her birth certificate. In 1933, the federal United States hypothecated all of the present and future properties, assets and labor of their "subjects," the 14th. Amendment U.S. citizens, to the Federal Reserve System (the non-federal Federal Reserve Bank).

In return, the Federal Reserve System agreed to extend the federal United States corporation all the credit "money substitute" it needed. Like any other debtor, the federal United States government had to assign collateral and security to their creditors as a condition of the loan. Since the federal United States didn't have any assets, they assigned the private property of their "economic slaves," the U.S. citizens, as collateral against the unpayable federal debt. They also pledge the unincorporated federal territories, national parks forest, birth certificates, **and nonprofit organizations,** as collateral against the federal debt. All has already been transferred as payment to the international bankers.

Unwittingly, America has returned to its pre-American Revolution, Feudal roots whereby all land is now held by a sovereign and the common people have no right to hold allodial title to property. Once again, We the People are the tenants and sharecroppers renting our own property from a Sovereign in the guise of the Federal Reserve Bank. We the People have exchanged one master for another. This has been going on for over eighty years without the "informed" knowledge of the American people, without a voice protesting loud enough. It is now easy to see why America is fundamentally bankrupt.

Why don't more people own their properties outright? Why are 90% of Americans mortgaged to the hilt and have little or no assets after all debts and liabilities have been paid? Why does it feel like you are working harder and harder and getting less and less?

We are reaping what has been sowed, and the result of our harvest is a painful bankruptcy and a foreclosure on American property, precious liberties, and way of life.

Few of our elected representatives in Washington,

D.C. have dared to tell the truth. The federal United States is bankrupt. Our children will inherit this unpayable debt, and the tyranny to enforce paying it. America has become bankrupt in world leadership, financial credit and its reputation for courage, vision and human rights. This is an undeclared economic war — bankruptcy and economic slavery of the most corrupt kind !"

END OF TRAFICANT SPEECH.

19
Two Factors Of Money

Money has two factors that define it — **intrinsic value** and a **fixed quality**. Everything that has these two factors is money, everything that does not, isn't.

Gold and silver have *always* been considered money, in all cultures, throughout the history of mankind. These metals meet the two conditions required of money and they're handy to use.

Every element, other than carbon, is money. Even water is money. The reason you don't see people carrying gallons of water to the store to pay for things is because water is not handy to use.

Diamonds are **not** money, *although they have intrinsic value,* because they vary in quality. Diamonds do not have a stable and fixed quality.

Federal Reserve Notes are **not** money, because they do not have intrinsic value. They cost two cents to make, regardless of denomination. The non-federal Federal Reserve makes $0.98 cents profit on every dollar bill printed, and a $99.[98] dollars profit on every $100 bill printed.

Assuming it is the government that does this (*actually it's not; the Federal Reserve is no more federal than Federal Express*), one might wonder **why** the government needs money in *taxes, license & permit fees, citations, fines and penalties and confiscations,* and all the other subtler methods it uses to take our property from us.

Federal Reserve Notes are **negotiable instruments** that discharge debt, **but they are not money.** They are not backed by silver, like they were in the days of the silver certificates, nor are they backed by any other **commodity** that meets the definition of money. The **collateral** for Federal Reserve Notes is the *"future" labor of the People of the United States* as evidenced by their Birth Certificates. One of the keywords to note is *"future."* In other words the collateral of labor doesn't exist now, it may exist later. So Federal Reserve notes are negotiable instruments called *promises to pay* or *"promissory notes."* They are *instruments of indebtedness ; — evidence of debt.*

We can no longer *pay our debts* because our *real money* has been removed from circulation. All we can do is *discharge our debts.* We do this with fake counterfeit, money. *Federal Reserve Notes are counterfeit money.*

Many other things have been replaced by their fake counterparts in the past few years. *Food* for instance. *Real maple syrup* comes from a maple tree. But the brown sugar-water, *a la chemicals,* that you are served in the House of Pancakes may *look like maple syrup,* but it isn't a product from a maple tree.

We used to have *real laws that apply to people* (*implementing regulations*)*,* rather than *fake laws that apply only to corporate fictions* (*statutes and codes; color of law*).

We used to have *real titles* to property, rather than *certificates of title* (*color of title: deeds*). If you *really* owned your land you would **not** be subject to property taxes or building codes. Since you only have a deed, the STATE owns your house and land, and if you don't pay your *yearly rent* (*property taxes*), the STATE will take your house and land away from you.

There is the *real,* and there is the *artificial.*

There are two **"States"** of whatever State you live in. One has hills and valleys and rocks and trees and dogs and cats and people in it. The other is a *government entity*, a *corporate fiction.* When you fill out a government form that asks **"Are you a resident of the State of Maine?"**

You presume to know what the *word* **"resident"** and the *phrase* **"State of Maine"** means, but you should be *certain* before you sign that legal document *under penalty of perjury.*

There are two of you, in the same way. The *real* and the *artificial.* The *real you* is created by God, and if somebody pinches you, you will feel it. The *artificial you* was created by the STATE as a corporate fiction.

Whenever you receive a letter from a creditor or debt collector, or the IRS, it is always addressed to your *all-capital-letter trade-name.* That's because the letter is *not* addressed to you, but to *your artificial strawman.* On your personal checks issued to you by your bank, *your strawman's name and address are imprinted in all capital letters* for the same reason. If a neighbor puts a letter in *"your" mailbox, that does not have a stamp on it,* he can be fined or imprisoned for trespassing on *government property.*

In the same way, your Birth Certificate has your strawman's name on it. *It too is government property.* The STATE owns that Birth Certificate, and your strawman. You may have a Certified copy, but the Original is on file in the *Bureau of Vital Records* (in the State in which you were born) in the *Department of Commerce,* because your **Birth Certificate** is evidence of you as the **collateral** that is backing **Federal Reserve Notes.** Your *Birth Certificate* is the STATE's **Certificate of title to you.**

How did you become chattel property of the State? The Constitution supposedly *forbids* slavery. By trickery and deceit the State created a corporate fiction (*your strawman*) with that Birth Certificate, and as long as you don't know the difference between *your strawman* and the *real you,* the least common denominator is *your strawman.*

When you're driving on the street, *perhaps at a higher speed than the posted speed limit,* but you haven't damaged any personal property or person. A cop can stop you, hand you a bill at gun point, and deny your rights to travel and to due process in one fell swoop, because the cop is not *dealing with you,* the real live human being, but *only with your artificial strawman.*

We were taught in public school that there are **three branches of government** — the **executive,** the **judicial** and the **legislative.** Well, where does the DMV, or the IRS, fit into that equasion? They don't. They're in the **artifical, fourth branch of government — administrative agencies.**

Administrative agencies would like you to think that they have legislative authority over you, which they don't. The only *authority* or *jurisdiction* they can claim to have over you is **in commerce, by contract over corporate fictions.**

The **real you** has God-given rights. It doesn't matter whether you live in a country with a constitution that supposedly protects those rights or not. You have **God-given rights** just by being you. The fake you, **the corporate fiction or strawman,** only has **"benefits" and "obligations" under contract,** and possibly, **diminishing "civil rights"** — poor substitutes for *real rights.*

Civil rights may be politically correct, but they are counter to nature and **God-given rights.** For instance, it may be a civil right not to be discriminated against because you have brown eyes, but the deeper (*real, God-given-*) right is the right to associate with anyone you want to associate with, and to **not** be forced to associate with anyone you don't want to associate with. If you don't want to hire brown eyed people, just because you don't like brown eyed people, that is your God-given right.

God-given rights include the rights to *livelihood, property, travel, due process, sovereignty, happiness* and *health.* These are not *privileges* provided by the STATE.

Knowledge *alone* is not power. The ***proper use*** of knowledge is power.

It is important to know the difference between the real and the fake, **and it is *essential* to know the rules by which we should live.** There are constitutional experts in jail because ***they contracted their God-given rights away in exchange for State privileges.*** It's important to be familiar with the Uniform Commercial Code (UCC) because it encompasses the ***real rules on planet Earth.***

One of the ***ten basic maxims*** of Commercial law is:

An unrebutted Affidavit is presumed to be true.

This means that whenever you get a bill, a fine, a penalty, assessment, or demand or presentment in commerce, it behooves you to ***respond to it timely,*** because if you don't — if you ignore it, you *acquiesce (silently agree)* to the truth of it. You loose your due process, and the presentment may not have been true in the first place.

The ***better*** way to play the **commerce game** is to ***respond timely*** and request that your adversary ***respond timely*** to you as well. Often times it is ridiculously easy to pull the rug out from under an IRS agent, or a debt collector, simply by making some righteous, formal request that they will not, or cannot respond to.

No law makes it mandatory for any real, live human being to pay income taxes, have income taxes withheld from one's pay, or even file a tax return? How could there be? This is an obvious fact. The Supreme Court has ruled very clearly that **when you file an income tax return, you are waiving your 5th Amendment Right to not testify against yourself.**

No law makes it mandatory that anyone waive any of his rights. Hence the *seldom used* statement, **"All Rights Reserved."**

When many people get an inquiry from IRS asking them where their tax return is, they panic and ignore the inquiry, and six weeks later they get an unsigned assessment that contains fines added in, and penalties, on the way to being levied or liened.

Actually, the IRS never sends out *real liens* - only **"Notices of liens"** — but they usually get the County Recorders to treat them as *real liens* anyway.

When you get a letter from the IRS asking you where your tax return is, you might write back very *humbly, simply and immediately,* and give them **Power of Attorney** to complete your tax return for you as long as they sign it **under penalty of perjury,** and you may never hear from them again.

Another way to illustrate using the maxim **"An unrebutted Affidavit is presumed to be true"** is also a way to explain terminating unsecured debt.

Banks do not issue loans. This is a shocker to many people because we are taught to believe that if we want a loan, we go to a bank. *But banks do not issue loans.* Banks are prohibited from loaning their customer's assets, or their own, because that would violate **GAAP (Generally Accepted Accounting Principles)**.

Banks are prohibited from loaning their own assets because that would violate Federal Reserve Regulations. What is left? *Nothing. Banks do not issue loans.*

When you leave the bank with a credit card application or any other type of so-called *loan application,* you are actually giving the bank your *promise to pay* them, by your *signature* on your *promise to pay.*

Your name is your bond. It could be on a piece of toilet paper, no matter. It is a *promissory note* that the bank **"cashes"** and then gives you a *deposit of equal value in return.* They don't disclose that there wasn't any real loan, or any risk, or collateral, on their part. They simply pay a clerk $12 an hour or so to make an entry on a computer pad. [This is what causes inflation; all so-called money is created out of thin air]. The banks violate usury and racketeering laws every day by charging you principle and interest on the *fictitious* so-called "loan".

One way to **terminate** this unsecured debt, without bankruptcy, is: when your **strawman** gets the bill, send in a minimum payment with a cover letter that says at the top **"Notice of Final Payment."** In this brief cover letter, make a formal request in commerce that they (*the so-called creditor*) answer your question, **"where was the risk or the collateral for that so-called loan?"**

Well again, *there was no loan; there was no risk, and there was no collateral.* They can't answer that question, and you end up creating a *new contract* in which your strawman doesn't owe them anything anymore. This *new contract* replaces the old contract in which your strawman might have owed them thousands of dollars. This *new contract* is called a lawful **"Novation."**

Evading responsibility is not being advocated here; **if you have made a mess, it is up to you to honorably clean it up.** But if the mess you've made is merely a *mirage,* or *masquerade,* it is appropriate to handle it by *mirage or masquerade means.*

Step by step, over the last few decades, the substance of our money, our laws, our rights and our freedoms have been overlaid by something resembling but counter to these precious things.

Our society has become a tyrannical police state. However, we can still be truly free because it is our birthright as human beings on earth — it just takes knowledge and action, to step out of the spell that has been cast over the common man by the conspiratorial powers that be.

The laying of the groundwork to one's freedom and sovereignty requires dotting all of the "i's" and crossing all of the "t's". . . *in at least three steps . . .*

1) . . . file a UCC-1 Finance Statement (*declaration*) to establish a public record that you are *not* the strawman, but are in fact the **"holder-in-due-course"** of it. This changes **the presumption of law** from the **public side** (*the State*) over to the **private side:** *your domain.*

2) . . . make yourself the Power of Attorney over your strawman. Level the field via your UCC-1 Finance Form.

3) . . . copyright your strawman's name. This gives you a very important offensive weapon, because from this point on, anyone who is coming after your strawman for anything **without your permission** is trespassing on your commercial property without **just compensation** to you.

Perhaps you've heard of the term **"judicial immunity."** That a judge has **"unlimited immunity"** by which a clerk, or a cop, or an IRS agent, is protected by his or her agency. Well, it hardly exists at all. **The only immunity that any agent has, exists within their jurisdiction.** They have no jurisdiction over you, the real live person, in your domain.

When you know the difference between who you are, and who you've been led to *believe* you are (*a corporate fiction*), and when you **effectively assert** this difference, the scales of justice are unlocked and the balance of power reverts back to you.

There is no money in circulation today — only credit.
Congress borrows FRNs from the non-federal Federal Reserve on the credit of the United States. Soverans are the source of the credit of the United States. Congress must return the credit to you when so claimed.
Your name is your credit bond.

20
Overcome Debt With Knowledge

The truth can set you free from your debts because there is no *real money* with which to pay them. A Federal Reserve Note is not *real money*; it is *legal tender* which *discharges* debt by transferring the liability to someone else. Most debts remain unpaid until Federal Reserve Notes are redeemed with substance backed money with which to pay them.

Federal Reserve Notes are *promissory notes of the United States* that Congress *promises to redeem* with our credit upon demand.

A *bill* is a demand for *real money* meaning substance (*silver or gold*) backed currency. A *bill* is a demand for *payment* that cannot be made because there is no *real money* with which to *pay one*.

Federal Reserve Notes in lieu of our credit *discharge* debt. Your credit (*your promise to pay*) will *extinguish* debt if you *accept the bill for its value with your credit sign* (your endorsement) *and return the value to the sender to settle the account.*

Congress borrows Federal Reserve Notes from the Federal Reserve Bank with bonds that accumulate interest for the Federal Reserve System backed by the *credit* that Congress borrows from the People of America making them preferred stockholders in the corporate UNITED STATES. The *credit* that Congress borrows from the People of America is called *"the credit of the United States."*

"Congress shall have power / to borrow money on the credit of the United States." — *Article 1, Section 8, clause 2, U.S. Constitution. [1:8:2]*

Congress borrows Federal Reserve Notes from the Federal Reserve Bank with bonds that are backed by *the credit* of the People of America. Federal Reserve Notes represent the United States corporation's promise to pay *real money of account of the United States* or its credit to the holders of Federal Reserve Notes upon demand.

Real money of account of the United States is currency backed by gold and silver coins manufactured in a United States Mint. (*Coinage Act of 1792*).

Federal Reserve Notes seem always to be in short supply. The United States must borrow more Federal Reserve Notes to cover the interest it must pay to the Federal Reserve Bank on the Notes it borrows, *ad infinitum.* There are never enough Federal Reserve Notes to cover the entire debt of the nation without borrowing more Federal Reserve Notes to cover the interest on the entire debt.

Federal Reserve Notes are *debt instruments* — evidences of debt that enslave us, *so why use them? The use of Federal Reserve Notes is optional.* Our slavery to Federal Reserve Notes is a *voluntary choice (whether we know it or not).*

In 1933, House Joint Resolution 192 made it a federal offense to refuse to accept Federal Reserve Notes (*promises to pay; **promissory notes***) to discharge, dollar for dollar, contracts demanding gold. HJR 192 of 1933 did not *order* people to use Federal Reserve Notes to discharge debt; it simply *allowed* people to use Federal Reserve Notes to discharge debt.

People use Federal Reserve Notes *voluntarily (whether they know it or not).* By using Federal Reserve Notes, people *volunteer into voluntary servitude* to the Federal Reserve Bank.

Since there is no *real money of account of the United States* a charge (*an invoice; a bill*) is an *offer to contract* to settle the debt with Federal Reserve Notes or a *mutual offset credit exemption exchange.*

The debtor has the *option* of **discharging** *the debt* with Federal Reserve Notes and enslaving himself to the Federal Reserve Bank by thinking that Federal Reserve Notes are real money that must be used; or **paying** *the debt* with his credit (*his mutual offset credit exemption exchange*) — if and when he knows that he can.

Here is the remedy.

Commercial Redemption is based on the fact that there is no **real money of account of the United States.**

During the previous century our legal system was converted from *common law* to *commercial law* by the owners of the Federal Reserve Bank. They **pretend** that there is **equal protection under the law** and that **involuntary servitude does not exist**, but these pretenses are not true.

They use legalese (*words of art*) to controvert the meaning of every legal document we sign. By using legalese the Bankers can say that they offer **equal protection under the law** and give **full disclosure of the material facts, without lying or stealing,** but do they really?

You and I do not know how to decipher their legalese so we seldom read the legal documents we sign. Due to our advisors — loan officers, attorneys, moms and dads, teachers and preachers — *and the overall mental conditioning of society* — we believe everything we hear and see on TV.

Without **full disclosure** *of the material facts* we believe everything we are told.

On May 23, 1933, Congressman Louis T. McFadden (R-OH), *Chairman of the House Banking and Finance Committee,* brought formal charges against the Board of Governors of the Federal Reserve Bank, The Comptroller of Currency, and the Secretary of the Treasury of the United States for numerous **criminal acts,** including FRAUD, UNLAWFUL CONVERSION OF MONEY, AND TREASON.

To protect themselves from these criminal charges the House and Senate (*both Houses of Congress*) passed House Joint Resolution 192 on June 5, 1933.

HJR 192 of 1933 states that the people who had surrendered their gold to the federal government in obedience to President Roosevelt's unconstitutional and illegal proclamation for citizens of the United States to surrendered their gold to the United States — were exempt from paying their debts since *their means of paying their debts* had been taken away from them and replaced with *money substitutes* — **fiat** Federal Reserve Notes that *discharge debt* instead of *paying debt*.

Public policy HJR 192 of 1933 provided a *REMEDY* for the victims of President Roosevelt's crime. This *REMEDY* is the basis of *debt cancellation by law* today.

In HJR 192 of 1933 the Board of Directors of the corporate UNITED STATES (*meaning Congress*) **confirmed, after the fact,** Roosevelt's removal of America's gold from circulation and its replacement with fictitious, substitute instruments of debt. This *CONVERSION* created the *EXEMPTION* upon which *debt cancellation by law is based.*

The debt cancellation process accesses a UCC contract trust account that the federal Government has been using in your name, since you were born, without your knowledge and consent to help pay the interest on the federal debt to the private non-federal Federal Reserve Bank.

They made the government the beneficiary of a *private constructive cestui que trust* and are using your *commercial energy* to fund the interest on the government's ever increasing federal debt to the private, non-federal Federal Reserve Bank.

The US Treasury created a *private constructive cestui que trust* through which the United States corporation and all its subsidiary corporations — *states, counties, cities, towns, school districts, fire districts, etc.* — interact with your *fictitious mirror image strawman.*

Fictitious corporations cannot interact with *the living flesh and blood woman or man;* they can interact only with the *fictitious mirror image strawman* that you are presumed to *accommodate* by performing and co-signing agreements in his name. They have convinced you — *the living flesh and blood woman or man* — that they are addressing you instead of your e*ns legis* (*government created*) *fictitious mirror image strawman.*

You are **presumed** to be voluntarily accommodating your *fictitious mirror image strawman* (whether you know it or not). The **debt** belongs to the **fictitious you** but the **real you** is **presumed** to be responsible and liable for the *fictitious mirror image strawman's* actions and debts.

Now that you are aware of this **presumption** you can redeem your status from government control **by rebuttal,** and stand **first in line, and first in time** to recover **dollar for dollar** the collateral the government has been holding in your name and earning interest on since you were born.

MAXIM: *He who has the gold pays the bills.*

In **Commercial Redemption,** a presentment (*an invoice; a bill*) is an offer to contract to discharge a debt. A bill or a debt is a liability or a *negative charge* (*a debt*) to your debtor strawman (*the debtor*) but a *positive charge* (*an asset*) offer of credit to *you* (*the secured party creditor of your strawman*). It is not a demand for credit from you.

Everything is reversed.

A bill to your strawman is an offer of credit to you . . . so why not accept **the credit offered to you** and pay your strawman's debt with a **mutual offset credit exemption exchange** between you and the presenter of the offer of credit, and thereby settle and close the account?

To do this simply endorse the presentment (*the invoice; the bill*) your strawman receives with your signature (**your credit sign**) and thereby acknowledge and accept the debt credit for its value and return its value to the sender as a *mutual offset credit exemption exchange* that settles, satisfies and closes the account.

Your **endorsement** of the charge — with **your name** (*your signature*), **your number** (*your Social Security Number*), and **transaction date** — transforms the charge into a **promissory note** which extinguishes the charge with your **mutual offset, credit exemption exchange,** when you return the extinguishing credit to the sender.

To confirm the dollar for dollar value of this exchange, make a postal money order *payment of consideration* for this contract. The claimant demanded **real money of account of the United States**, and you offered to pay the full **dollar for dollar value** of the debt with your **mutual offset, credit exemption exchange.** If the claimant **refuses to accept your offer,** his refusal puts him in dishonor and default; and in **contempt of congress!**

His refusal to accept your **legal tender offer** puts him in violation of **public policy HJR 192 of 1933** which **requires** his acceptance of a legal tender offer *or he forfeits his right to his claim.* The claim then rebounds upon him (*the respondent*) because he **dishonored** your offer to pay him with **real money of account of the United States** (*when such is restored*) so he must discharge his claim himself.

The only way to educate creditors in the commercial redemption principles is to demonstrate that their demands for **real money of account of the United States** must be withheld until **real money of account of the United States** is made available again.

The creditor has the same **equal opportunity** as you to wake up and *stop playing the fiat money game.*

Accept and Return. *Accept* the value of the charge and *Return* the value of the charge to the sender, extinguished.

The only money you have to extinguish a debt with is your credit — *the constitutional credit of the United States* — *your mutual offset credit exemption exchange.*

21

Equity Interest Recovery

During the financial crisis of the Great Depression of 1929-1933, the **tangible substance of real money** (gold and silver) was removed from the monetary system of the United States.

In its place the **intangible substance** of the American people (*the wealth and productivity that belongs to them*) was pledged by the government as collateral for the debt, credit, and currency of the UNITED STATES, and placed at risk so Commerce could continue to function. This is well documented in the actions of President Roosevelt and Congress and in the Congressional debates that preceded the execution of reorganization measures in bankruptcy.

"The new money (paper Federal Reserve Substitutes for real money) *is issued to the banks in return for Government obligations, bills of exchange, drafts, notes, trade acceptance, and banker's acceptances.*

"The new money will be worth 100 cents on the dollar, because it is backed by the credit of the nation. It will represent a mortgage on all the homes and other property of all the people in the nation." — Senate Document No. 43, 73rd Congress, 1st session.

This new money belongs to *"all the people in the nation."*

The National Debt is defined as *"mortgages on the wealth and income of the people of the country."* — Encyclopedia Britannica, 1959. The people's wealth is their income, productivity, and private property.

The **bankruptcy reorganization** of the UNITED STATES is evidenced by 1) the Emergency Banking Act of March 9, 1933, 2) House Joint Resolution 192 of June 5,

1933, and 3) the Series of Presidential Executive Orders that surround them.

Twenty years prior to this on December 23, 1913, Congress passed *"An Act to Provide for the establishment of Federal Reserve Banks to furnish an Elastic Currency to afford a means of rediscounting Commercial Paper and to establish a more effective Supervision of banking in the United States and for Other Purposes"* called The Federal Reserve Act.

One of the *"other purposes"* of the Federal Reserve Act was to authorize the *hypothecation* of the obligations of the UNITED STATES which the Federal Reserve Banks were authorized to hold under 12 USC 14(a). An *hypothecation* is a *"pledge of property as security or collateral for a debt without delivery of title or possession."* — *Federal Reserve Act, section 14(a).*

A *tacit hypothecation* is a hidden lien or mortgage on property that is created *by operation of law* without the parties express knowledge or agreement creating a *tacit mortgage* or *tacit maritime lien*. A *tacit hypothecation* is a *hidden taking of assets* owned by a party other than the taker to be used as collateral for a loan without transferring the owner's title or use to the taker.

If the *owner of the assets* that the *taker takes* and uses as collateral for a loan retains the possession and use of the property, but the bank (*the lender to the taker/borrower*) can take and sell the property in the event that the borrower (*the taker of the assets*) defaults on the loan, the action is called *in words of art* a *pledge of assets* to the taker.

If the *taker of the assets* pledges the assets to a bank as collateral for a loan, the process is called *(in words of art)* a *re-hypothecation*. In either a *hypothecation* or a *re-hypothecation* there is equitable risk to the actual owner of the assets.

Federal Reserve Notes are *"obligations of the United States"* to the American people and the Federal Reserve Bank. — *Federal Reserve Act, section 16; codified at 12 USC 411.*

"The full faith and credit of the United States" is the **substance taken from the American people by hypothecation**, the real property, wealth, assets and productivity of the people that has been *re-hypothecated* to the Federal Reserve Bank by the UNITED STATES for its obligation to the Federal Reserve and US issuance and backing of **borrowed Federal Reserve Notes** as legal tender *"for all taxes, customs, and other public dues."*

In other words, the **hidden taking of the assets** of the American people to be used in Commerce by the UNITED STATES while leaving the people with possession and use of those assets is called *in words of art* an **hypothecation**. If the *taker of the assets* (**the US**) pledges the same assets to a *bank* (**the FRB**) as collateral for a loan the procedure is called *(in words of art)* a **re-hypothecation**.

In either a **hypothecation** or a **re-hypothecation** equitable risk and interest accrues to the owners of the assets (*the American people*), therefore **Federal Reserve Notes are <u>priority obligations</u> of the United States <u>to the American people</u> and <u>secondary</u> obligations of the United States <u>to the Federal Reserve Bank</u>**.

The commerce and credit of the people of the united States of America continues today under the **bankruptcy reorganization of the UNITED STATES** as it has continued since 1933 backed by the **assets and wealth of the American people** at risk for the federal government's obligations, currency, and Federal Reserve Notes.

Under the 14th amendment, and numerous Supreme Court precedents, and in equity, the private property of the American people cannot be taken or pledged to the UNITED

STATES for public use and put at risk *without due process of law and just compensation* (*remedial recovery of equity-interest*).

The UNITED STATES cannot pledge and risk the property and wealth of the people of America for any government purpose *without legally providing them with REMEDY* to recover the equity-interest that is due them on their risk. Courts have long ruled that to have one's property legally held as collateral or surety for a debt, even when one still owns it and has the use of it, is to DEPRIVE the owner of his property since it is at risk and could be lost for the debt at any time.

The United States Supreme Court said that the Constitution provides that *"private property shall not be taken for public use without just compensation."* (*United States v. Russell, 13 Wall, 623, 627*).

The *owners* of the assets are presumed to be *subrogated* to the *taker* and therefore liable for the taker's payments on his bank loans. *Subrogation* is the substitution of one party for another whose debt the party pays, i.e. the sovereign is presumed to be substituted by the government created strawman.

"The right of subrogation is not founded on contract. It is a creature of equity, enforced solely for the purpose of accomplishing the ends of substantial justice, and is independent of any contractual relations between the parties." — *Memphis & L.R.R.Co. vs. Dow, 120 US 287, 302-302 (1887)*.

The *American people who own the assets and originating credit are presumed to be subrogated to the corporate UNITED STATES* and therefore liable for Congress' interest payments to the non-federal Federal Reserve on the Lawmaker's borrowed and ever increasing National Debt.

Under the *laws of equity*, the United States of America cannot hypothecate and re-hypothicate the property and wealth of its private citizens and put it at risk as collateral for its currency and credit with the Federal Reserve Bank or any other bank without legally providing them with an equitable REMEDY for recovery of what is due and payable to them *upon demand.*

The United States government does not violate the law nor the Constitution by doing this in order to collateralize its financial reorganization under bankruptcy to the Federal Reserve Bank because the United States government does in fact provide a legal REMEDY for the recovery of what is due to them as accrued interest for risking their assets and wealth, so that it can legally hypothecate and re-hypothecate the private wealth and assets of the people who back its obligations and currency with their substance and credit and their implied consent.

The provisions for the REMEDY are found in **Public Policy HJR 192 of 1933** (a.k.a. Public Law 73-10) that *suspended* the gold standard for US currency and *abrogated* the right to demand payment in gold, and made Federal Reserve Notes legal tender for the first time, *"backed by the substance or credit of the nation"* — i.e. backed by the **substance and credit** of the People of America.

All US currency since 1933 is only CREDIT backed by the real property, wealth, assets and future labor of the sovereign People of America, taken by *presumptive pledge* by the UNITED STATES and *re-pledged* for a *secondary obligation* to the Federal Reserve Bank.

The sovereign American people cannot recover what is due them by anything drawn on Federal Reserve Notes of debt without expanding their risk and obligation to themselves, because any recovery payments backed by this type of currency (*negative FRNs*) would only increase the public debt that they are collateral for, which in equity would not satisfy anything, but which the REMEDY in equity is intended to reduce, because there is no longer *actual money* of substance with which to pay anybody anything.

There is no *actual money* in circulation today by which debt owed by one party to another can actually be paid.

Although declared legal tender for all debts public and private in the bankruptcy reorganization, Federal Reserve Notes of debt can only *discharge charges of debt*, whereas debt must be *payed with substance,* i.e. gold, silver, barter or some commodity, *and extinguished.*

For this reason the "Public Policy" of our current monetary system (HJR 192 of 1933) uses the technical term **"discharge"** as opposed to **"payment"** in laying out Public Policy for the monetary system of this New World Order, because *a debt cannot pay a debt ;* a negative charge cannot neutralized a negative charge it just increases it.

Ever since 1933, Commerce in the corporate UNITED STATES and among its sub-corporate entities has been conducted only with negative instruments of debt, i.e. debt note instruments by which the liability of a debt is *discharged* and transferred to someone else, in a different form, but never *extinguished* until lawful, substance backed *"money of account of the United States"* is restored.

The unpaid debt created and expanded by the current Monetary plan carries a **"public liability"** for its collection, because when debt is discharged with debt instruments in Commerce (*FRNs included*) the debt is expanded instead of extinguished, thus expanding the public debt — a situation eventually fatal to any economy.

Congress and the government officials who devised the public laws and regulations that orchestrate the bankruptcy reorganization of the corporate UNITED STATES, anticipated the long term effect of the *debt based monetary system* that many in government feared, which we face today in servicing the interest on trillions upon trillions of "dollars" of US *negative corporate debt,* so government officials made statutory provisions for REMEDY to provide *equity-interest-recovery* and satisfaction to their Sureties (*sovereign Americans*), and at the same time *alleviate,* if not *eliminate* the National Debt problem as well.

Since the real property, wealth and assets of all Americans is the **substance** backing the obligations, currency and credit of the UNITED STATES, such **credit** of the UNITED STATES is tacitly offered, and can be used for **equity-interest recovery** *via mutual offset credit exemption exchange.*

The legal definitions written by Congress relating to legal tender provide for *private unincorporated people* to issue promissory notes for **equity-interest-recovery** on their risk by the lawful tender payment of legitimate debts in Commerce as REMEDY due them in the financial **reorganization in bankruptcy** now in effect; ongoing since 1933.

Public Policy HJR 192 of 1933 provides for the discharge of every obligation "dollar for dollar" of and to the federal UNITED STATES by discharging the obligations that *private unincorporated people* owe against the same dollar for dollar amount of obligation that the UNITED STATES owes to them thus providing a REMEDY for orderly **equity-interest recovery** and the eventual cancellation of the corporate, public debt.

The public debt is that portion of the total federal debt that is held by the public. — *31 USC 1230.*

Public Policy HJR 192 of 1933 (Public Law 73-10) and 31 USC 5103 gives the *Secured Party Creditor of the UNITED STATES* the right to issue legal tender promissory notes **"upon the full faith and credit of the UNITED STATES"** as obligations of the federal UNITED STATES. For these reasons, no creditor can require tender of any *specific type of currency* in place of **promissory notes** tendered in good faith for legitimate debt.

The REMEDY for **equity-interest recovery** *via mutual*

offset credit exemption exchange is codified in statutory law even though ***mutual offset credit exemption exchange*** is virtually unknown and seldom utilized in Commerce today.

22
The Money Trust

There are at least three administrative procedures that can be used to eliminate debt.

One way to eliminate debt is to file a commercial lien against your money trust.

In our money system there are no funds because there is no real money. The government uses your strawman's name and your credit to create a trust account at the FRB and the IRS (*with themselves as trustees*) and use that trust account as collateral on the *federal debt,* in an asset account, after it is monetized in the money market of the world.

Filing a commercial lien against your money trust establishes your right as the trustor (*the source of the credit*) and takes the trust back under your control so you can transfer trust credits to offset the trust debits of the account thereby discharging the debt.

You must realize that the debt is not *your* debt personally. It is *your strawman's* debt. You have been functioning as a voluntary representative for that **cestui que trust account** (*your strawman*) by *discharging your strawman's* bills with fiat money instead of *paying* them with your *mutual offset credit exemption exchange.*

When you established your first checking account, you unknowingly accepted this relationship with the trust that the government established in your name. You have not had control of this trust because you have never claimed it and your parents could not control it for you because they were wards of the state, like you.

The System maintains the illusion by artifice and deception design.

Look at your checkbook.

How do they present your name? As an ALL CAPS NAMED business CORPORATION. Try to have them change that **title** to a normal, caps and lower case name. They cannot because their data bank input will not allow it. The bank personnel will not know why but they will insist on the ALL CAPS NAME of the CORPORATION that the bank presumes you to be.

A clue to that presumption is in the line on your checks over which you sign your name. The **microprint signature line.** It's not a line. It's printed words, some of the finest printing you will ever encounter. It says something like: AUTHORIZED REPRESENTATIVE AUTHORIZED REPRESENTATIVE AUTHORIZED REPRESENTATIVE AUTHORIZED REPRESENTATIVE (etc., etc.)

In the corporate world, only the **authorized representative** of a CORPORATION has the authority to sign the corporation's checks. So you, *the human being,* have been given the *authority* to sign the checks of *your money trust* (*your strawman*) which is an incorporated entity that is a fiction.

For more than 125 years corporations have had many of the attributes of human citizens. By creating a fictitious entity that has the attributes of a *living person in law,* they deceive the *real human being,* whose name they have taken from his Birth Certificate.

The Birth Certificate is a Manufacturers Certificate of Origin (MCO) in the hands of the government that is *pledged* on the National (*federal*) Debt.

The IRS is the collection agency for this pledge. The foundations of the IRS are its parent corporations, the FEDERAL RESERVE BANK (FRB) and the INTERNATIONAL MONETARY FUND (IMF), to collect on the bankruptcy debt instruments that they hold.

This all caps name (*your strawman's name*) is how the US Corporation, State corporations, County corporations, and School District corporations communicate with you, through this supposedly CORPORATE YOU.

When you place a *commercial lien* against the COR-PORATE YOU *for what it owes* **you** for paying its bills to cover what the government **owns in your name,** you take back the birthright power that the government usurped from you at your birth.

The Constitution says that the government cannot levy a direct tax on the Citizens of a State, so they don't. They instead levy a tax on the *corporation which they created* and therefore control (**your strawman**) and send the bill to your **residence** confident that you will never figure this out and that you will **voluntarily** pay for what the government **owns in your name,** that you do not own but are permitted to **use** — as long as you obey the rules of this Socialist System of today.

As in *The Matrix,* you are trapped in a system that *extracts your energy* through your strawman (*a fiction*) and fools you into thinking that that fiction is you.

As long as you partner with that fiction (*the CORPORATE YOU*) they control the *real you* (*in many ways*). You are *chattel* (*cattle*) for their purposes.

Your children can be taken away from you to be sent off to *fight in contrived wars* and to *bow to the System's demands.*

It's all Commerce.

This is why **the flag of the Ship of State** displayed in public places has a gold braid and trim, and is why witnesses testify in court the **"dock."** Admiralty courts administer the Laws of Commerce in the Queens Colonies beyond the sea.

Yes! The system does not want you to break free, but when you take the necessary steps to claim the difference between *you* (*the real person*) and the *fictitious person* (*your ens legis strawman*) they can no longer expect you to pay the bills assessed to your *strawman* (*the fiction*) for what the government owns because you have claimed (*on the record*) that the government fiction (*your strawman*) owes you interest for the CREDIT that the government has borrowed from you all these years, so before anyone gets paid for your strawman's debts, you *get reimbursed* instead.

Your lien is a commercial lien on a *debtor entity* (*your strawman*). You are following the REMEDY the System established for you to claim your independence from State control.

It's not *your* fault. It's not *your* National Debt either. The fault lies in the **malfeasance** and **misfeasance** of government because they took the REAL money away through fraud and left you with no subtantial means to pay your bills, only to discharge them.

When you agree to the terms of any bank loan or credit card, *you* (*the living human being*) create the **money** for what you need with your *signature* (*your credit sign*).

The private FEDERAL RESERVE BANK deposited the *"money" that you created* to the government's account and demands that you pay the interest on the *"money" that you created* until you have acquired sufficient debt instruments (*federal reserve notes of debt*) to exchange for the discharge of the fictitious debt.

That credit card is not yours. Look at the ALL CAPS NAME on the card. The debt is owed by the *fiction* even though you have the *use* of the services and goods.

The fault lies in a Congress that was coerced, cajoled, or complicit in **extorting energy** from you, and intentionally or unintentionally squandering away your **heritage** and the past and present *future heritage* of your family.

When you *finally* take responsibility for yourself instead of remaining a ward of the state, you *mark your maturity as a real human being who is a* ruler over the government instead of being its *subject.*

23

The New (debt free) World Order

Welcome to the New (debt free) World Order
Debt is one of the biggest worries for most families and businesses. The information that is presented in this textbook can help to set you free from debt forever through *debt elimination.* Not debt *consolidation* nor debt *management,* but *debt elimination.*

Debt elimination is real, and thousands of people just like you and me have taken back their lives through *debt elimination.* The process is legal and ethical. It draws on the *insurance bond* that was established to compensate for the wealth of each American that is consigned as collateral on the national debt — **Public Insurance Policy HJR 192 of 1933.**

You can take control of your **corporation-of-one** (*your government created strawman*) as is your legal birthright.

There are none more hopelessly enslaved, than those who falsely believe they are free.

When you don't *know* your rights, you don't *have* any.

When you don't know how to *secure* your rights, you don't have any.

Only when you *know* your rights and how to *secure* your rights do you have rights and are sovereign.

When you don't know that you are *rich,* you are *poor.*

When you **know** you are rich, but don't know how to **secure your assets** you are **still** poor. Only when you know you're rich and *secure your assets* are you *rich.*

You have been *convinced* that you borrowed therefore you *owe.* You assumed a *voluntary servitude* that is not required of you by law, and you were *not informed of this* by the party responsible for this deceit.

There has been no *disclosure of the material facts* by the bank or credit card company, that they had *nothing to give you* in return for the obligation to them you assumed. They convinced you to unknowingly **give them your property** in exchange for your own credit back.

It was not the bank's money that bought you your home. You did not receive any value from them. Your **promissory note** supplied the credit for the loan transaction. In return for your **promissory note** (*your credit*) they leased your credit back to you as rent for thirty years and hold the title to your house for having supplied nothing to the transaction in return.

What's more, your **promissory note** was sold many times *without your knowledge or consent* even though your **promissory note** still belongs to you. In *monetizing your* **promissory note** the bank increased the bank's wealth by nine or ten times the value of the **promissory note** and demands that you pay them back *the principal of the note plus interest* on the credit by **promissory note** that you provided when you applied for the loan.

We have been engaged in commerce on a *promissory-note standard* instead of a *gold standard* since 1933.

Congress buys Federal Reserve Notes from the Federal Reserve Bank with bonds backed by the credit of we the People of America. The credit that Congress borrows from we the People of America is called **"the credit of the United States."**

"Congress shall have power / to borrow money on the credit of the United States." — *Article 1, Section 8, clause 2, U.S. Constitution.*

Federal Reserve Notes represent the United States' promise to pay interest to the Federal Reserve Bank on these notes.

Your ***promissory note*** created money that the so-called lenders gave back to you as an alleged "loan." The Bill of Exchange that they gave you (*the bank check*), for say a $120,000.⁰⁰ loan, is worth more than $1,000,000.⁰⁰ to the bank when monetized on the Discount Exchange Market.

As a "thank you" for giving the bank the ability to use your ***promissory note*** to vastly increase the assets of the bank, the bank expects you to pay back the $120,000.⁰⁰ principle you received as *your credit, in changed form,* plus the interest you pay the bank on the non-loan over thirty years, which nearly triples the cost of the mortgaged property.

And you unknowingly **give** them the collateral of the house that you paid for at the start with your ***promissory note,*** should you default. Are you still worried about your moral position in the deal?

In the "mortgage" process we describe, there is no *contract from the beginning*. A "mortgage" is not a contract at all (*just as the Constitution of the United States is not a contract at all*). A contract requires two parties, an **offeror** and an **acceptor** (*an offeree*) who at the time of the contract's acceptance (*its creation*) agrees to be bound by the contract terms as evidenced by the signatures of *both parties* to the deal.

Every *mortgage lender* intentionally obtains his customer's ***promissory note*** by *non-disclosure, concealment,* and *suppression of the material facts* that the *mortgage lender* is not risking any of his own assets in the transaction, and that the *mortgage lender* intentionally obtained his customer's ***promissory note*** by concerted action, with full knowledge of the end results of his individual participation in *fraud, larceny,* and *conspiracy to defraud,* in contempt of the RICO act.

A *mortgage lender* is not a party to a mortgage under the laws of contract. No agent or principal of the *mortgage lender* will sign a mortgage contract because he is fully aware that the *mortgage lender* is not tendering any **consideration** to bind the transaction.

Therefore, having provided no **consideration** and having shown no intention to be a party to the contract by signing it, neither the *mortgage lender* nor any *third party who may purchase the mortgage at a later date,* has any **legal authority** to enforce the terms of the mortgage. Therefore, the **mortgage contract** fails for lack of consideration **and is void.**

There is no **power of attorney** stated in the mortgage granting the *mortgage lender* the legal right to use the individual's **promissory note** for the *mortgage lender's* personal financial gain, without compensating the *maker of the* **promissory note**.

There is no written, *granted authority, or disclosure* stated in the mortgage for the mortgage lender or any other *party,* to *pool, encumber, pledge, hypothecate, or trade* the applicant's **promissory note** on the secondary market where all trades are cleared by the Federal Reserve and are **off the books trades,** without compensating the *maker of the* **promissory note**.

You, *the maker of the* **promissory note** in the mortgage "contract," gave no representative status to any agent or principal of the mortgage lender. After obtaining the **promissory note** the *non-authorized actions* of the mortgage lender, regarding the applicant's **promissory note,** creates the *implied obligation* for him to disclose the material facts of the transaction to the maker of the note.

If the mortgage were actually a **contract,** then the mortgage lender would have tendered **consideration** and have in his possession the **original unmarked and unaltered note** in order to sell the note or enforce the mortgage contract. This is why the contract is **void for fraud.**

When the *mortgage lender* obtains the customer's **prom-**

issory note without consideration on his part, the *mort-gage lender* commits **constructive fraud** by acts of concealment of the material facts. These acts concealing the material facts establish a **breach of contract** since the mortgage lender has the legal duty to act in good faith and disclose all material facts to the *mortgagee* relative to the transaction.

Having obtained the customer's **promissory note** by **constructive fraud,** the *mortgage lender* is not justified by any *implied consent on the part of the customer* to enforce the contract, as true consent implied or otherwise cannot be given under a cloud of non-disclosure, concealment, and suppression of the material facts, or a state of duress.

If the *soveran* has the rights of sovereignty over himself and his property, then each *soveran* is capable of entering into a social contract. But by the use of the mortgage, the *soveran* is deceived into **use by privilege** of what he thinks he has as **ownership by right.**

A *privilege* is granted by an authority, whereas a *natural right* is granted by God, implying *ownership.*

The 14th Amendment to the Constitution of the United States places the *soveran* under the protection of the United States CORPORATION that administers the District of Columbia and all other *federal territories* and *possessions.* So the *mortgage lender,* the *lawyer,* and the *judge* take advantage of the *soveran* under the *undisclosed (hidden) presumption* that the individual is a *perpetual child who is incompetent and a ward of the state;* not legally capable of entering into any contract, while yet enforcing an *implied* contract.

Are you still concerned about your moral stature?

A contract creates the law.

A contract is a living body of law that is an agreement made between living people with their full knowledge and voluntary consent. When a contract's sponsor uses words and terms that convey privileges and authority which he has no right to convey, *it is fraud.*

The moral issue is the banking industry's long term practice of *constructive fraud* by breach of contract, nondisclosure, and *larceny as well.*

Your moral requirement is to uphold your right to be deemed considered a *soveran* instead of a *subject.*

At this moment, you are considered by law to be in need of an attorney to represent you. Your government employees have taken your substance without permission as collateral for the a debt that they have created. Since you have not said *"I am capable of accepting responsibility,"* you are treated as though you *are irresponsible.*

You seek licenses to be granted by your government employees as though they are the Lord of the Manor, and in seeking *privileges* from them, you confirm their *presumption* that you are a subject of the State. They presume that *since you have not taken control of your own affairs,* you are content to remain under their care.

So morally, *to avoid the issue (of status),* you allow the governments to usurp power from you and from all other soverans who are unaware that they have surrendered the status they held under the constitutional Republic to the military Democracy called the State.

By default, *you and all others who are unaware, have created the present dictatorship by your failure to act in your own accord.*

24
Non-adversarial Novation

Banks rarely go to the trouble and expense of attempting to sue someone who stops paying on their strawman's credit card that the bank owns. When they *know* that you know that it is *your* credit not *theirs,* and that they have *violated federal law,* it's unlikely that they will file suit. They must obey the regulations in *consumer protection laws* that prevent *predatory lending.*

There are *two different procedures* for handling credit card debt. One for those who are not in default or in danger of default. Another for default judgments, takings, court cases, liens, collections, and debt collection attorneys.

The *non-adversarial approach* is comprised of three different ways to use the administrative processes of the Uniform Commercial Code (UCC) for those who are not in default or in danger of default.

1. You can file a commercial lien against a UCC contract trust account at the US Treasury which gives you status as the *superior, first in line first in time secured party creditor.* By making claims within the *national bankruptcy* you can extinguish your debt with your *mutual offset credit exemption exchange,* and reduce the National Debt.

2. You can dispute the legality of the lending process.

3. You can apply the *administrative process of Novation,* which works under federal banking laws and deals with *default judgments, takings, court cases, liens, collections,* and *debt collection attorneys,* wherein they must abide by their statutes, or they lose.

Credit Card Dispute / Novation Contract Offer

The purpose of this administrative procedure is to discharge credit card debt and update your credit record using the established procedures of common contract law: the *Uniform Commercial Code*, the *Fair Debt Collection Practices Act*, and the *Fair Credit Reporting Act.*

Novations Under The Law

A *novation contract* is a new agreement which is recognized in the law.

NOVATION (civil law): - the substitution of a new debt for an old debt whereby the old debt is extinguished by a new debt contracted in its stead.

A Novation substitutes a new debt and a new agreement for the contract claimed by the credit card company. Almost every credit lender uses the novation procedure.

Any time you get a notice of an **update** to the terms and conditions of your credit card agreement, this **update** is in fact an **offer** to enter into a *Novation* (*a new contract*). When you use your credit credit card after receiving the new **update,** you agree to the new terms of the Novation. Your **act** of using the credit card demonstrates your **acceptance** of the new credit card agreement. How else could they change your credit card terms without your openly expressed approval and consent.

Insurance companies use this *novation procedure,* also, such as when you have a claim for $20,000.^{00} for damages and they send you $3,000.^{00} instead, trusting that you will accept this payment without quams.

Credit Card Dispute And Novation

You can use the novation procedure to enter into a new agreement with a credit card company, *under your condi-*

tions and terms, by making the credit card company an offer that the credit card company can accept with an act.

Send the credit card company a check for some nominal amount (*say $20 or $25*) with the stated condition that by accepting the tender it agrees to your new *conditions and terms* (*your novation contract*). When the credit card company accepts the check by cashing it, it has accepted your novation contract as well. If they return the check without cashing it, repeat the process with a U.S. Postal Money Order, instead, which they have to accept as enforced *legal* tender.

This procedure is designed to bind the credit card company to the terms and conditions of your Novation contract which include but are not limited to . . .

a) cancellation of all previous agreements;

b) admission that the debt is **"paid as agreed"**;

c) waiver of all claimed right of arbitration against you;

d) obligation to report the disputed account to credit reporting agencies as **"paid as agreed"**;

e) agreement to not take any collection activity against you and to inform any assignees of the account that it has agreed that the account is **"paid as agreed"**;

f) the requirement that it *verify in writing under penalty of perjury* any amount of debt that you allegedly owe;

g) agreement that any breach of the terms of the Novation contract by them will injure and damage you and make the alleged collector liability for damages.

Upon notice, a Novation contract binds any and all collection agents of the credit card company and third party collection companies relative to your Novation contract. Your Novation contract establishes a legal basis for declaring invalid all allegations of debt made against you that are associated with the credit card account and sent through the U.S. Mails.

Your Novation Contract establishes a legal basis for claiming injuries and damages should the credit card company or any collection agency breach the terms and conditions of your Novation contract.

Your Novation contract destroys any legal basis for the credit card company or any collection agent to ignore your card dispute and Novation contract by your . . .

a) . . . choosing and use of a procedure permitted and recognized by contract common law, the Uniform Commercial Code, the Fair Debt Collection Practices Act, and the Fair Credit Reporting Act;

b) . . . establishing the card company's obligation and third party collector's obligation to *verify under oath* the amount of any debt that they allege you owe;

c) . . . removing any controversy between your demand for verification of any alleged debt and any and all presentments by third parties containing unverified allegations of debt against you;

d) . . .removing any presumption that you willfully avoided a known debt.

Legal Precepts Behind The Credit Card Dispute And Novation Offer

In every legal dispute, one side is deemed to have the **presumption of truth** and the *other* side is deemed to have the **burden of proof.**

When a person is accused of a crime, the law presumes that he is innocent until proven guilty beyond a reasonable shadow of doubt. In contract law, a party is presumed to have entered into a contract (*in this case by an implicite act*), knowingly, willingly, and for an exchange of *consideration,* upon full disclosure of the facts.

A claimant cannot accept the **benefits** of an offer without accepting the **obligations** attached to the offer. (*Aetna Investment Corporation v. Chandler landscape & Floral*

CO., 227 Mo.App. 17, 50 S.W.2d. 195, 197 and In re Larney's Estate, 148, Misc. 871, 266 N.Y.S. 563).

By sending your Novation offer and notice of dispute, supporting your offer with *consideration* in the form of a check made out to you credit card company for $20-$25 you declare . . .

a) . . . the consequences of the card company's acceptance of your offer;

b) . . . the legal basis for claiming zero liability for any alleged debt of a prior agreement once your offer is accepted;

c) . . . the adverse consequences to the card company of any collection activity that does not contain *sworn verified proof* of your obligation as a debtor.

Credit Card Compnay Responses

To provide proof of any debt liability, the debt collector must provide a **sworn verification** of the amount of *lawful money loaned to you,* and that his claim arose from a signed contract which supersedes your Novation contract.

Pursuant to the Fair Debt Collection Practices Act (15 USC 1601) and the terms and conditions of your Novation contract, any subsequent collection attempt that does not include a **sworn verification of debt** will result in an admission that you have no liability regarding the account in dispute.

You will probably receive an invalid response, consequently the debt collector's default and breach of your Novation Contract, thereby setting the debt collector up for a claim for damages against him.

Clearing Up Your Credit Report And Legal Concepts Behind Credit Reporting Bureaus' Fiduciary Duties

The *BIG THREE* credit reporting bureaus — EQUIFAX, EXPERIAN, TRANSUNION — keep personal information on your credit worthiness. They are ***third party suppliers*** of that information and have a ***legal duty*** to assure its accuracy, and a ***fiduciary duty*** to keep it accurate as well. Their ***fiduciary duty*** is your friend indeed.

Once it has been established that your credit card company has knowingly and willingly entered into a Novation contract with you, you have a legal basis for requiring the credit bureaus to *designate your account **"paid as agreed."***

Send a *sworn notice* with *verified evidence* and a *demand to the credit reporting bureaus* that they remove all negative information from their records concerning you unless the debt collector provides the credit reporting bureaus with VERIFIED PROOF that your Sworn Notice to *the credit reporting bureaus* is inaccurate or false.

Such proof is impossible, as you have already established and shown the credit reporting bureaus that there is no evidence available or forthcoming that would overcome and outweigh the evidence of the Novation contract. Consequently, due to the fiduciary duties of the credit reporting bureaus, under common law and their obligation under the Fair Credit Reporting Act, the credit reporting bureaus have a legal obligation, and duty — if they receive no verified evidence to overcome and outweigh your Sworn Notice of Novation contract — to *designate* in their records that the account with the credit card company is ***"paid as agreed."***

They must correct the records no later than 30 days after receiving your Sworn Notice.

25

Loans Of Credit

Credit lenders flourish today because of interest payments.

You, as the borrower, are the original source of the principle amount of any alleged loan, by virtue of your *promise to pay* (*your application for credit and promissory note*), from which a *negotiable instrument* is made (*credit money per UCC 3-104*), which the credit lender converts into another form, be it a cashier's check, a bank draft, or a bank account deposit that is issued to you as a so-called *loan.*

This *loan* is nothing more than accounting digits entered on the bank's computer pad. The bank loans nothing of substance to you and is forbidden by the banking regulations of the non-federal Federal Reserve Bank from loaning any assets of the bank, or the bank's depositors' funds.

"Loans" that end in default are simply charged off, i.e. *discharged by a bookkeeping entry,* with no loss incurred by the bank or its depositors, which is precisely why the Redemption procedure is effective in nullifying loans of credit from lending institutions and banks.

The bank has no valid, verifiable risk in any loan transaction and therefore no valid claim; because it only loans you your credit.

The Fair Debt Collection Practices Act

The FDCPA, codified at 15 USC 1692, stipulates that a debt collector must validate the alleged debt *if he is requested to do so,* and he must *cease all collection activity until validation is provided.* Validation (*or verification*)

Connect The Dots And See! 197

is defined as *confirmation of correctness, truth, or au-thenticity, by sworn affidavit, oath or deposition.*

"Affidavit of truth of matter stated and object of verification is to assure good faith in averments of statement of party." — Black's Law Dictionary, Sixth Edition, 1990.

The debt collector must swear true, correct, and complete — *(the equivalent of the truth, the whole truth, and nothing but the truth, i.e. testimony)* — that an **exchange of valuable consideration** has occurred that allows him to demand repayment *in kind.*

Banks do not loan substance, only credit, *thin air.*

No Bank attorney and no Banker can validate a loan of substance, hence they are foreclosed (*estopped*) from issuing a relevant affidavit.

The banking system is fraudulent by nature so it cannot be made legitimate by a false affidavit.

The only person who can validate a debt is the borrower himself. This is why the IRS prosecutes for *failure to file a tax return* because *a 1040 Form signed under penalty of perjury, and sworn to be true, is your validation of the debt.*

The IRS is a *debt-collection agency* and debt-collection agencies cannot prosecute a debt unless they have some **statement from the taxpayer** validating the debt.

Loan Snapshot: From Credit Lender's Perspective

When you apply for a $100,000.^{00} bank loan, you sign a $100,000.^{00} *promissory note* that funds the $100,000.^{00} bank deposit to your bank account that you receive.

What is the actual *cash value* of your *promissory note*? It is $100,000.^{00} because the bank sells your *promissory note* for $100,000.^{00} in government bonds, which have an equal value to cash. The lender merely exchanges actual cash value for actual cash value and you are charged as if it is a loan of money to you.

The Federal Reserve Bank of San Francisco publication entitled *"Monetary Policy in the United States"* says that *"bank loans are funded by banks creating new deposits."* (p.13)

The bank claims that it is a *loan,* but it is a *quid pro quo (value for value) exchange* they deceptively *call* a loan. The proof is in the bookkeeping entries according to GATT.

No actual cash value was paid by the bank for your *promissory note* but your *promissory note* funded the bank loan deposit that you received.

If you give the bank $100.^{00} in cash as collateral for a bank loan, and the bank deposits the $100.^{00} cash and uses it to fund a $100.^{00} loan to you that you would have to repay, and the bank refused to return the $100.^{00} cash to you, when you payed off the loan, it would be theft.

That is exactly what the bank does on every *loan of your credit* it makes to you. When you give the bank your *promissory note* it has an equal value to the loan deposit the bank gives you in return.

Who paid for your promissory note?

When a bank grants a $100,000.^{00} loan all they are doing is taking $100,000.^{00} cash value from *you* (*via your promissory note*) and transferring it to *themselves* as a gift — for free.

The bank did not loan one cent of the bank's money or their depositors money to obtain your $100,000.^{00} *promissory note.* They posted your *promissory note* on the bank's books as a deposit from you to the bank and used the $100,000.^{00} they obtained from you, via your *promissory note,* to create the $100,000.^{00} checking account deposit they gave to you.

The checking account deposit they give you has the

equivalent value of legal tender because your ***promissory note*** can be sold in the money market for legal tender.

The bank uses the *newly created checking account deposit* to fund the $100,000.^{00} *checking account deposit* they give to you to be repaid to them at interest!

Isn't it about time that we free ourself from the bondage and fraud of mortgage companies and banks?"

26
Nothing Covered Not Revealed

"There is nothing covered, that shall not be revealed; and hid, that shall not be known." — *Matthew 10:26.*

Here is a moral position that can no longer be hidden from view.

Since 1933 the US CORPORATION has been bankrupt, therefore real money is no longer available to pay our debts, only *debt instruments* that when used to discharge our debts *increase the national debt* at the same time. Having no **substance** in commerce, only **our credit** can *extinguish* our debts per **our surety bond bill of exchange,** *our mutual offset credit exemption exchange.*

We own nothing and have the **privilege of use** at the sufferance of the State.

By *switching positions* with you, the mortgagor became the *acceptor of your offer* and ends up **owning the mortgage agreement in-due-course.** As **holder-in-due-course,** the bank obtains the **right of ownership** and you receive the **privilege of use.**

When any title is registered the State becomes the owner of the property — the car, house, boat, etc., — and you must pay **rent to the feudal lord** for the **privilege** of the **use of your property,** *and for its tax liability, its license fees, its maintenance, etc.*

Similarly, getting a marriage license, a driver's license, or even a dog license, establishes **state ownership** and **user privilege, as well.**

As in the case of a serf, who is required to obtain permission from the Lord of the Manor to join with a mate in conjugal bliss, — (*where the first right of intercourse goes*

Connect The Dots And See!   201

*to the Lord of the Manor so that the children will be con-
sidered his)* — the marriage license legally assigns *all
"produce" of the partnership* to the State *as a first right.*
You obtain the **privilege** *of companionship and having
children* but not as **holder-in-due-course of the right** *to
nurture, protect **and own them** as you see fit.*

The State can decide whether or not children can be
raised by their parents or taken from them and placed in
foster care **as wards of the state.** Once in *foster care*
many of the children then **mysteriously disappear.**

This is the system you support by your non-action, — by
not establishing your right to the **substance** which has been
taken from you *without your knowledge or consent.* We
must learn to take back the power we inadvertently let slip
away.

This is not your fault. The schools, attorneys, the media,
the government, the banks, do not provide us with the
informationwe need to make informed decisions to protect
our family and ourselves. This however does not diminish
our responsibility to become informed.

Now that you have a clearer idea of what is at stake you
may *now* realize some of the **consequences** of being un-
informed. You have the choice of *pretending that things
are too complicated to be understood,* — or to reform your
ways. The choice is up to you.

Freedom comes not from guns nor the ballot box.

Many of my friends have been supporting elective can-
didates to try to make a difference in this country, to bring
it back to the **visions** we were taught in school, the images
and ideals that were instilled in us as children and the sto-
ries we were told about our nation and its founding.

Much of that **false picture** has slipped away with both
Democratic and Republican leadership.

Something is terribly amiss, for we can't seem to halt

the plunge toward the totalitarianism of fascist dictatorship.

A few years ago I would have *agreed* with my friends and swung into action to help elect *"the lesser of two evils."* But that is not my solution now.

The 2000 election showed clearly that federal elections are manipulated and the 2002 election put the icing on the cake.

I've engaged in conversations with *Mr. Sheeple* and I recognize in *his* mental programming, *my own.* The lie of choosing the *lesser of two evils* is seductive and effective indeed. We are now citizens of a *military democracy* instead of the founding *republic of peace* and we attempt to defend our freedom by our electoral participation; *but this too is a lie.* It's a scam.

We get so busy fighting each other, over seething *emotional* issues, that we don't notice that choosing the *lesser of two evils* assures us a continuance of the lie.

"There are a thousands hacking at the branches of evil, to the one striking at the root." — *Henry David Thoreau.*

How does one strike at the root? You've heard the aphorism, *"money is the root of all evil."* Well it's truer than you might think.

Mayer Amschel Bauer, *who founded the Rothschild dynasty, and took its name,* said:

"Give me control of a nation's money and I care not who makes its laws."

His son, Amschel Mayer Rothschild, said:

"Permit me to issue and control the money of a nation, and I care not who makes its laws."

Another son, Nathan Mayer Rothschild bragged:

"I care not what puppet is placed upon the throne of England to rule the Empire on which the sun never sets. The man who controls Britain's money supply controls the British Empire; and I control the British money supply."

Rothschild's sons learned well. Do you get the picture? They didn't waste their time with **federal election politics.** They understand the **real levers of control.**

For more than 300 years the Illuminati — comprised of the world's richest families, *the international bankers and financiers* — have been playing both ends against the middle by implementing wars in which armaments and men are needed on both sides.

The financing for these great expenditures comes from the international bankers and financiers.

War weakens all countries involved, and the Illuminati step in to buy up property for pennys on the dollar, and influence. When the wars are over, armaments must be replaced and the devastation of war must be repaired.

The international bankers and financiers make money in the beginning, in the middle, and in the end.

They control the law-makers of the country, the courts, and the media, by controlling the money system.

They control the schools and universities through foundations and gifts.

They have stolen the country and are now seeking total control of the world.

So will you hack at the branches or strike at the root?

Take back your power. Cancel the illegal contracts you've been conned into agreeing with and signing. Eliminate mortgages legally and morally. Eliminate credit card debt. *Use your credit,* credit the US government has been using as collateral against its enormous debt, *instead of you.*

Your *commercial credit* (*your birthright*) has been stolen and misappropriated *and you've never been told that it exists.*

By *presumption,* the US government has held you bodily as collateral for their wasteful spending on wars and oppressive conquests fought in your name!

You've been *praying for peace* - while *paying for war.* You've been *paying for war* and the cruel oppression of others - while *praying for peace.*

You have a choice to legally end the *dilemma* that has been forced upon you.

Are you concerned about the morality of eliminating your debts via the established law?

By accepting the *illusion* that banks loan you *their* money instead of loaning you *your credit* instead, you have fallen into the trap of *supporting oppression and endless war.*

Vote with your "money." Take back the *credit* you unknowingly let the government use your whole life.

Take back the *energy* you have loaned the government them that allows them to load the dice against peace.

Find out how and act now!

New Beginning Study Course

27

What Can We Do?

All of our money is created out of debt; it is a debt-money system. Our money is initially created by the purchase of bonds that some day have to be repaid.
The public buys bonds (*like savings bonds*). The banks buy bonds. Foreigners buy bonds. When the Fed wants to create more money in the system, the Fed buys bonds — but pays for them with simple **book keeping entries** which it creates out of nothing. This **new money,** created by the Fed, is then multiplied by the Fed and its member banks, **by a factor of nine or ten,** via the fractional reserve scam.

Although the banks don't create currency *per se,* they *do* create **check-book-money** by the stroke of a key *or by deposit accounts,* by making new loans.

The Fed even *invests* some of the money that it creates out of nothing but thin air. In fact, over one-trillion dollars of this *privately created money* has been used to purchase bonds on the open market, which provide the banks with roughly fifty billion dollars **in risk free interest each year,** less the *minor* interest banks pay to depositors.

In this way, *through fractional reserve lending,* the banks create more than 90% of the money supply and almost all of the country's inflation.

What can we do about this?

Fortunately there is a way to fix this, easily, speedily, and without any serious financial problems.

We can get our country totally out of debt in one to two years by paying off these U.S. Bonds with debt-free U.S. Notes, like the notes Lincoln issued to pay for the Civil War.

This by itself, however, would create tremendous inflation since our currency is presently multiplied by a factor of nine or ten by the fractional reserve banks. *But there is a simple solution* (advanced in part by economist Milton Friedman) *to keep the money supply stable and avoid inflation and deflation while the debt is being retired.*

As the Treasury buys back it's bonds on the open market with interest free United States Notes, *the reserve requirement of the many banks would be proportionately raised, according to law,* so the amount of money in circulation is held constant.

The bonds being paid off in U.S. Treasury Notes, would be deposited in the banks, thus making available the funds the banks need to increase their reserves. Once the U.S. Bonds are retired with U.S. Notes, banks would be at *100% whole reserve banking,* instead of the *fractional reserve system* currently in place today.

From this point on, the buildings of the former Fed would only be needed as central clearing houses for checks and as vaults for the U.S. Notes.

The Federal Reserve Act would no longer be necessary and could be repealed. Monetary power would be transferred from the FED to the Treasury Department. There would be no further expansion nor contraction of the money supply by the banks.

By controlling our monetary system in this way, our national debt would be paid off in a single year, or two, and the Fed and fractional reserve banking would be abolished without national bankruptcy, financial collapse, inflation or deflation, nor any significant change in the way the average American goes about his business.

For the first time since the Federal Reserve Act was passed in 1913 taxes would begin to go down until no longer needed at all, as a real blessing to the average American.

28

Four Steps Of Money Reform

Elements Of A Monetary Reform Act

Now let's take a look at these proposals with a *Money Reform Act* in mind. Variations, with the same results, would be equally welcome of course.

STEP 1. Pay off the national debt with debt-free U.S. Notes, *or Treasury department credits convertible to U.S. Notes.* As Thomas Edison put it:

"If the U.S. can issue a dollar bond, it can issue a dollar bill. They both rest purely on the good faith and credit of the U.S. This amounts to a simple substitution of one type of government obligation for another. One bears the cost of interest, the other does not."

Federal Reserve Notes could be used for this as well, but could not be printed after the Fed is abolished as we propose. We suggest using U.S. Notes instead, as Lincoln did.

STEP 2. Abolish Fractional Reserve Banking. As the debt is paid off, the reserve requirements of all banks and financial institutions would be raised proportionally at the same time to absorb *the new U.S. Notes* (to prevent inflation), which *would be deposited and become the banks' increased reserves.* At the end of the first year or so, all of the national debt would be extinguished, and we could start enjoying the benefits of *full-reserve banking.* This same approach would work equally well in Canada, England and in virtually all other debt-based, central bank controlled economies.

STEP 3. Repeal of the Federal Reserve Act of 1913 and the National Banking Act of 1864. These acts delegate the money power to a *private banking monopoly.* They must be repealed and the monetary power handed back to the government (*in the U.S.: the Department of the Treasury*) where they were *initially* under President Abraham Lincoln. No banker nor person in any way affiliated with financial institutions should be allow to regulate banking. After the first two reform staps, these Acts would serve no useful purpose anyway, since they relate to a fractional reserve banking system.

STEP 4. Withdraw the U.S. from the **IMF**, the **BIS** and the **World Bank**. These institutions, like the Federal Reserve, are designed to further centralize the power of the international bankers over the world's economy. *The U.S. must withdraw from them or lose its sovereignty and independence.* The harmless, useful functions they supply, such as *currency exchange,* can be accomplished either nationally or in new organizations limited to those functions.

Issuing debt-free currency, not tied to bond issues, is not a *radical* solution. It's been advocated in its parts by Presidents Jefferson, Madison, Jackson, Van Buren and Lincoln. It's been used at different times in Europe as well.

One current example is one of the small islands in the English Channel off the coast of France. **Guernsey** has been using issues of debt-free money for nearly 200 years to pay for large building projects. **Guernsey** is an example of just how well a debt-free money system can and will work.

In 1815, a committee was appointed in **Guernsey** to investigate how best to finance a new market. The impoverished island could not afford more new taxes, so the

State's Fathers decided to issue their own paper money. They were just colorful Paper Notes backed by nothing at all, but the people of this tiny island agreed to accept them and trade with them anyway.

To ensure that the Paper Notes circulated widely, they were declared to be *"good for the payment of taxes."* Of course this idea was nothing new. It was exactly what the colonists in America had done before the American Revolutionary War, and there are *other* examples of this being done successfully throughout the world.

But this was *new to Guernsey,* and it worked. The market is still in use, and it was built *with no debt to the people of this island state.*

So what if America follows Guernsey's example?
The resulting advantages would include . . .

    1) . . . no more bank runs;

    2) . . . bank failures would be very rare;

    3) . . . the national debt would be entirely paid-off;

    4) . . . the monetary, banking, and tax systems would be more efficient, and simplified;

    5) . . . significant inflation and deflation would be eliminated;

    6) . . . booms and busts would become insignificant;

    & 7) banker control of our industry and political life would end.

How would the bankers react to these reforms?

Certainly, the international bankers' cartel would oppose all reforms that do away with their control of the world's economies — as they have in the past.

But it is equally certain that Congress has the Constitutional authority and the responsibility to authorize the issuance of **debt free money — U.S. Notes** the same as *Lincoln's Greenbacks* — and to reform the very banking laws it enacted on ill advice.

Undoubtedly, the bankers will claim that issuing debt-free money will cause severe inflation or make other dire predictions to frighten the People, but remember **the culprit — fractional reserve banking:** *the cause of almost all inflation* — not whether debt-free U.S. Notes are used to pay for the government's costs.

The simultaneous transition to **full reserve banking** will absorb the new notes and thus prevent inflation, while stabilizing banking and the economy as well.

In the current system, any spending excesses on the part of Congress, are turned into more U.S. debt bonds. The 10% of bonds purchased by the Fed, that provide the liquidity in the capital markets needed to purchase the remainder of the new bonds, is multiplied ten times by the bankers, causing most of the inflation we see.

Educate yourself and your friends.

"When you know a thing, recognize that you know it, and when you do not — know that you do not know: this is knowledge." (Confucius).

"You shall know the truth, and the truth shall make you free." (Jesus of Nazareth, the Bible, NKJV at John 8:32).

Our country needs a solid group who really understand how our money is manipulated and what the solutions are, because, now that a severe depression has come, friends of the bankers are coming forward advancing *so-called* solutions framed by the bankers.

Beware of calls to return to a gold standard. Why?

Simple; because never before has so much gold been so concentrated in foreign hands. Never before has so much gold been in the hands of international government bodies such as the World Bank and International Monetary Fund. In fact, the IMF *now* holds more gold than any central bank in the world.

The Swiss are under intense pressure from the Money Changers to dispose of their gold. This is most likely either a prelude to the complete *demonetization of gold* (*like silver before it*), or to its monopolization and remonetization by the Money Changers.

Therefore, to return to a gold standard now would almost certainly be a false solution in this case. As we said in the Great Depression: *"In gold we trusted; by gold we were busted."*

Likewise, beware of any plans advanced for a regional or world currency — **this is an international banker's Trojan Horse with which to conquer the world** — a deception to open the national gates to more international banker control.

Educate your members of Congress; it only takes a few persuasive members of Congress to make the others pay attention. Most Congressmen just don't understand the system. Some Congressmen understand the system but are influenced by their bank stock ownership or bank PAC contributions to look the other way, not realizing the gravity of their ignorance and neglect.

There is great opportunity for significant monetary reform at present. In this crisis, they at least now have been given the information needed to avoid floundering in banker-induced confusion, *as did many reform-minded Congressmen during the Great Depression.*

We pray that this coverage has made a useful contribution to the national debate on monetary reform. It remains for each of us to do his duty today, consistent with our status in life. May God give us the light to help reform our nation and ourselves.

We say ourselves: because ultimately vast numbers of us are going to be driven *more and more* to desperation by the accumulation of the world's wealth in fewer and fewer hands. We will be tempted to become *selfish and greedy* like our oppressors.

Rather, let's keep in mind this warning to not lose sight of the greater things.

As Jesus of Nazareth put it *ages ago . . .*

"For what will it profit a man if he gains the whole world, and loses his own soul?"

"Forgive us our debts as we forgive our debtors."
— Jesus the Christ, at Matthew 6:12.

Chapters 19 to 25 (revised)
duplicate
3 AMERICANS 51 to 57
published in
Epistle to the Americans III: What you don't know
about Money

Chapters 26 & 27 (revised)
duplicate
2 AMERICANS 31 & 32
published in
Epistle to the Americans II: What you don't know
about American History

— — —

Epistle to the Americans I: What you don't know
about The Income Tax
http://tinyurl.com/yfplutf

Epistle to the Americans II: What you don't know
about American History
http://tinyurl.com/yzme458

Epistle to the Americans III: What you don't know
about Money
http://tinyurl.com/yzuffbe

— — —

Monitions of a Mountain Man: Manna, Money, & Me
http://tinyurl.com/ygtkak8

Maine Street Miracle: Saving Yourself And America
http://tinyurl.com/yg9q8mm

Commercial Redemption: The Hidden Truth
http://tinyurl.com/yj4otn4

Connect The Dots And See!   217

Made in the USA
Middletown, DE
26 May 2024

54909643R00126